THE FIRST RETIREMENT MODEL
FOR CAREER WOMEN

PROJECT RENEWMENT™

Bernice Bratter and Helen Dennis

Illustrations by Lahni Baruck

□ □ □

Scribner

New York   London   Toronto   Sydney

SCRIBNER
A Division of Simon & Schuster, Inc.
1230 Avenue of the Americas
New York, NY 10020

First Scribner hardcover edition March 2008

SCRIBNER and design are trademarks of
Macmillan Library Reference USA, Inc., used under license
by Simon & Schuster, the publisher of this work.

For information about special discounts for bulk purchases,
please contact Simon & Schuster Special Sales:
1-800-456-6798 or business@simonandschuster.com

Book design by Ellen R. Sasahara
Text set in Electra

Manufactured in the United States of America

1   3   5   7   9   10   8   6   4   2

Library of Congress Cataloging-in-Publication Data
Bratter, Bernice.
Project renewment™ : the first retirement model for career women / by
Bernice Bratter & Helen Dennis ; illustrations by Lahni Baruck. — 1st Scribner
hardcover ed.
p.   cm.
1. Women in the professions—United States—Retirement. 2. Women executives—
United States—Retirement. 3. Women employees—United States—Retirement.
4. Retirement—Psychological aspects. 5. Self-actualization (Psychology).
6. Retirement—United States—Planning. I. Dennis, Helen.
II. Title. III. Title: Retirement model for career women.
HD6054.2.U6B73 2008
332.024'0140820973—dc22   2007032242

ISBN-13: 978-0-7432-9948-0
ISBN-10:   0-7432-9948-5

Project Renewment is a trademark of Bernice Bratter and Helen Dennis.
Photo credit: p. vii, Photographer's Choice—Nino Mascardi/Getty Images

We dedicate this book to
the extraordinary women of Project Renewment

and
To Edward Kaufman with love and appreciation

and
In loving memory of Lloyd B. Dennis

We delight in the beauty of the butterfly, but rarely admit the changes it has gone through to achieve that beauty.

—MAYA ANGELOU

CONTENTS

⊡ ⊡ ⊡

Introduction   1

Part I
Essays   15

1. Retirement: Yes or No   17

2. I Won't Earn Another Dollar   21

3. Change Is the Norm   25

4. What Is Productivity Anyway?   29

5. I Only Cry at the Movies   33

6. Who Am I Without a Business Card?   37

7. Addicted to Power   41

8. Less Steam in My Engine   45

9. Work *and* Retirement?   49

10. Feeling Vulnerable   53

11. Antiaging or Pro-Aging   57

12. Is Busy Better?   62

13. More than the Blues   66

14. Back to the Kitchen   71

15. Going It Alone   75

16. Passion: It's More than a Fruit   80

17. You Can Always Volunteer   84

18. What Do I Wear When I Am Not in
   a Business Suit?   88

19. Grandchildren: Finding the Balance   92

20. The Queen of Multitasking Is Taking a Break   97

21. Dealing with Illness   101

22. Personal Planning: Is It for Me?   105

23. What if *He* Retires First?   109

24. Play   113

25. Buying the Plot   117

26. Forever Guilty   122

27. Sex: Lest We Forget   126

28. I Lost My Keys and My Car   130

29. Pushing Sixty   135

30. Losing a Mate   140

31. Honoring Our Wisdom   144

32. The Illusion of Freedom   148

33. Connecting to My Soul   153

34. I Can Leave My House, but Not My Hairdresser   158

35. Joy   163

36. With a Little Help from My Friends   167

37. A Sorority House, Not a Nursing Home   172

38. Authenticity   177

Part 2
A Guide to Creating a Project Renewment Group
181

Appendixes

A: Acknowledgments   207

B: Women of Project Renewment (1999–2007)—
Partial Listing   209

C: Survey Data from Project Renewment Groups   210

D: New Member Survey   211

E: Follow-up Survey   212

F: Websites   216

G: Books of Interest   229

Notes   230

INTRODUCTION

◨ ◨ ◨

If you are (or were) fully engaged or passionate about your work and are thinking about retirement, this book is for you. If you want to create a future that is equal to or better than your past, read on. If you believe that financial security is only one aspect of success, read even further. And if you have never been satisfied with the status quo, you will find this book a good read.

In October 1999 Bernice Bratter, who was the executive director of the Los Angeles Women's Foundation, called her longtime colleague Helen Dennis with a question. "Has anything been done about career women who are facing retirement?" Helen, whose specialty is aging, employment and retirement, indicated little if anything had been done in this area. After a four-hour lunch, we decided that there was a lot to discuss about issues facing women who love their work, are considering retirement and want to figure out what is next.

We decided to have a dinner and invited friends and friends of friends who were successful career women. These women realized they had given little thought to their retirement and were eager to discuss their personal interests, concerns and fears. At that first dinner meeting, Project Renewment was born. Today, groups of career women in Southern California gather regularly to learn from one another as they create their future.

WELCOME TO PROJECT RENEWMENT

Renewment is a term we made up. It is a combination of *retirement* and *renewal,* an alternative to the term "retirement," which is still associated with negative stereotypes and clichés. In contrast, Renew-

1

ment is positive, suggesting rebirth, choices, vitality, opportunity and personal growth. It implies that decisions about the next chapter of life can be intentional rather than defined by the needs and expectations of others.

Project Renewment refers to a process, one that defines the dynamic changes that occur when women transform the drive and energy they previously committed to a career into a source of energy to re-create their lives. It also is a forum that provides a safe, small-group environment for women to explore issues and concerns related to retirement and post-career living. The women who participate are proactive, nonjudgmental and supportive. They discuss their priorities, losses and passions to intentionally design a future that will be equal to or more gratifying than their previous working years. Topics typically discussed include identity, relationships, money, health, productivity and defining what is meaningful during this new life stage. (Please see page 197 for a comprehensive list of topics and trigger questions.) Ultimately, Project Renewment is action-based, as each woman makes decisions about her future when the time is right.

We decided to put to use what we learned from those early meetings. Project Renewment is not a traditional support group, although women are supportive of one another. It is not a venue primarily to make new friends. But because of the shared mission, values and vision, new friendships have developed—one of the wonderful unintended outcomes of Project Renewment.

A LITTLE HISTORY

From its inception, our women made two commitments. One was their desire for personal growth and the other was an interest to develop a body of knowledge and experience that would benefit other like-minded women. This book is based on the collective and shared experiences, wisdom and knowledge of these women.

At that first meeting, the women made an instant connection as they openly discussed their insights, thoughts and feelings about retirement. Their professions were diverse: a market researcher who owned her own business for thirty years, a computer-systems analyst who did extensive expert witness work, a newly retired executive vice president of human resources, a clinical psychologist who just moved to Southern California, a newly retired women's studies and theology professor, a gerontologist specializing in aging, employment and retirement, a business consultant and two executive directors of nonprofit organizations.

We realized we had a group of enormously talented women with strategic planning capabilities to create and grow a new organization or business. But that is not what we wanted to do. We just wanted to meet regularly to explore issues, intelligently think about our future and share our experiences about this new part of our lives. In fact, we were so emphatic about not wanting to get too organized we decided to omit food assignments for our next potluck dinner meeting.

As a result, the menu for the next meeting was less than colorful. The meal was completely white: several pasta salads, white dinner rolls, cheeses and Krispy Kreme doughnuts for dessert. We decided we had overcompensated for our obsessive organizational behaviors and that food assignments were not a sign of strategic planning.

To capture discussions and keep us focused, we taped and transcribed our meetings for several years. We knew we were embarking on something new and different that might be useful to other career women. Most of the quotes in this book are based on those transcripts.

As word got out about Project Renewment meetings, other professional women asked to join. Since it can be difficult to sustain a group if new people continually join, we helped women establish a second group in January 2001.

Despite our efforts not to expand, the groups multiplied. The proliferation occurred through word of mouth; professional women heard about the meetings and wanted to be part of them. With our assistance, seven groups have been established consisting of eight to ten women each who meet monthly to discuss their careers and dreams for the future. Additional groups are forming.

Over time, these seven groups have evolved into small enduring communities of highly effective, caring women. They understand the concerns, complexities and contradictions of this time of life for themselves and for others. As one woman said, "We are approaching this next chapter of our lives in a conscious way instead of letting things just happen."

WHO ARE THESE RENEWMENT WOMEN? (SEE APPENDIX B)

Although there is nothing "average" about Project Renewment women, they do share some common characteristics. Based on a survey, the average woman in Project Renewment is married and in her mid-sixties. She is or was fully engaged and committed to her career and is likely to be managing some combination of part-time work and volunteer obligations. She wants to give back by volunteering, but prefers occasional volunteer commitments rather than regularly scheduled ones. At this point in her life, she is most concerned about changing health, replacing work with meaningful activities, achieving and/or maintaining financial security, feeling fulfilled and allowing herself to have fun. Her top priorities are staying fit, pursuing cultural/intellectual/creative activities, traveling, finding ways to give back to her community and spending time with family and friends. She rates her overall feeling about life as "very satisfied."

Here are some more specific results taken from the survey.

- The average age of women in Project Renewment is sixty-six, ranging in age from fifty-three to eighty-one years.
- About 70 percent of the women are married, 21 percent are single/divorced, 5 percent are single/widowed and the remaining 5 percent are single/other.
- Almost all (98 percent) love(d) or enjoy(ed) their work.
- One out of five Renewment women work full-time; half are self-employed and half work for others.
- Over one-third consider themselves "retired."

- More than one-third indicated their health has affected their ability to work and/or participate in other activities in the past year.
- More than half of the women are moderately concerned about their financial security and roughly one-third are interested in paid employment.

These women are working or retired attorneys, theatrical producers, newspaper journalists, teachers, executive directors, professors, systems analysts, social workers, small business owners and psychologists, to name a few. Their collective experiences and insights constitute a plethora of role models for all career women approaching their future. Despite the diversity of their careers, these women have a similar drive to create and optimize their own future. (See Appendix C for additional survey results.)

IMPACT

Project Renewment has had a positive affect on women's lives, as expressed in the following comments.

- "The most meaningful benefit of Project Renewment is being with a group of smart, insightful and compassionate women who are dealing with issues of retirement, aging and finding meaning in life."
- "The most meaningful aspect for me has been the opportunity to observe other women who are not working who have successfully used their new freedom to grow in new directions. I sense opportunities for growth and exploration all around me and I am now much more open to new experiences. I feel like a sponge!"
- "My participation in Project Renewment has helped me to not only accept the idea of retirement from the (paid) working world, but to value immensely this time of my life."
- "Project Renewment has opened my mind to important issues that I now can face in a more thoughtful way than I did before.

It provides a structure to review the changes and transitions in life that come one's way."

- "I am stimulated by the rich dialogue among the members and the conversations about lives lived, current interests, trends and future plans. After each meeting, I walk away feeling that I have gained something special. This is truly a commitment in which I receive much more than I give."

- "The group gives me an opportunity to test ideas and emotions which I am experiencing and to discuss them with a group of women I respect. It is a nonjudgmental setting and gives me a safe place to express feelings that I might not share elsewhere. I have learned so much from the wisdom and courage of the others."

- "I've expanded my perspective and achieved greater comfort about whatever will come next through the generosity and brilliance of my Renewment group. We have also forged wonderful friendships!"

- "Project Renewment gives content, structure and information to this transitional period of my life. It helps to have companionship in uncharted waters. I have gained by hearing others' experiences."

- "The group provides a sounding board and safety net of women I respect and can relate to. I now have role models and I recognize the endless possibilities in this life stage. I realize it is okay to fail."

- "Project Renewment has given me the opportunity to be introspective and take the time to think about reinventing and reinvesting in myself. It continues to inspire me and gives me permission to explore new things."

THE CASE FOR PROJECT RENEWMENT

For the first time in history, millions of highly effective career women face retirement. We are educated, skilled and successful. With our hard work, capabilities and commitment, we have achieved rewards beyond money. We have achieved visibility, respect, status and influence, and have made a difference.

Our generation of women is unique. We are the first cohort to live before and after the launch of the Women's Movement. And we are the first and largest generation of women to define ourselves by our work.[1] Because we are the first, we have few role models for retirement. According to Nan Bauer-Maglin and Alice Radosh, co-editors of *Women Confronting Retirement*, we have a new "population of women who face retirement and are unsure of their worth without their job."[2] This uncertainty has become a driver to create a retirement model that takes into account our unique connection to work and our values, preferred lifestyles, ideal relationships and what is important to us at this stage.

TIMES ARE CHANGING

Boomers have been identified as responsible for changing the concept and meaning of retirement. What has been somewhat ignored is that those of us in the preceding generation, the so-called Silents, have been quietly initiating the revolution. The power of Boomers must be acknowledged. As the largest generation in history—78 million born between 1946 and 1964—they cannot be ignored. Forty million are women.[3] And among these women, nearly one in four graduated from college.[4] Over one-third works in management, professions and related occupations.[5] About ten million are likely to work in occupations that provide rewards beyond money.[6] As they approach this new life stage, Boomers (men and women) are changing their focus from "success to significance," many hoping to recapture their youthful idealism and belief once again that a single individual can create change in the world.[7] And in that shift, the older or leading edge Boomers born between 1946 and 1955 are facing retirement concerns similar to those of the generation that precedes them—the Silent Generation.

Accomplished women such as former U.S. Supreme Court Justice Sandra Day O'Connor, actresses Elizabeth Taylor, Mary Tyler Moore and the late Natalie Wood, founder of the Children's Defense Fund, and civil rights lawyer Marian Wright Edelman, and divas Aretha Franklin and Barbra Streisand sprang from the Silents. Political leaders Geraldine Ferraro and Patricia Schroeder and domestic mogul Martha Stewart are among those who blossomed.

THE WOMEN'S MOVEMENT

In the 1960s Betty Friedan in her book *The Feminine Mystique* described a population of women who felt trapped and invisible. Her first chapter, entitled "The Problem That Has No Name," described women's feelings as "empty . . . incomplete . . . as though I don't exist."[8] "You wake up in the morning and there is nothing to look forward to."[9] The women were asking, "Is this all?"[10]

Women from the Silent Generation were the most prominent feminists leading the women's movement.[11] The consciousness-raising groups inspired by Friedan were the backbone of the movement in the 1960s and 1970s. They addressed women's problems of not getting out of the house often enough, becoming exhausted from caring for their children and yearning for job opportunities.[12] Women have moved beyond these issues, having "been there and done that."

It was Friedan who gave a voice to the Silents. And as the Silents matured and evolved, they established identities in addition to their marital, domestic and child-rearing roles. Friedan established the launching pad for career women of today. And yet as the clock moves forward, we wonder again how we will define ourselves, this time in retirement. "Is this all there is?"

We grew up learning to serve our families and the larger society first, and only after that were we allowed and sometimes encouraged to focus on ourselves.[13] As "other directed" women, we did what was expected from us—plus more.

We married, raised children, were supportive of our husbands' careers and moved as their jobs changed. Many of us returned to school and launched our own careers. Others remained single and accomplished their career goals through hard work while maintaining involvement with friends, family and the community. Divorced and separated women dealt with complexities and disruptions in their lives and still maintained family ties while establishing careers. We became the queens of multitasking, wanting it all and striving to have the best of all worlds.

The Silent Generation of women has matured and now faces a new challenge: to create a retirement model that mirrors our achievements and passion for work. It is a model that encourages us to focus on ourselves without ignoring the future of our families, communities and nation.

Financial security is fundamental in making the retirement decision, but money is only part of the story. Retirement for the Silents and very likely the Boomers is a new life stage that again raises questions about purpose, significance and identity in life.

For career women accustomed to life in the fast lane, the uncertainties can be unsettling. Filling our lives only with busyness can be a self-imposed barrier to growth. For our Project Renewment women, busyness has not been sufficient. Fulfillment, growth, joy, challenge and satisfaction have meant more than having a full calendar. The question "What do you do now that you are retired?" should be changed to "Do you love the life you are living?" Although our passions and priorities may change, our desires to feel productive and engaged do not.

MEANING OF RETIREMENT

If retirement had a single definition and meaning, knowing how to live the best retirement life might be easy. Retirement has many meanings that do little to serve as a guide. Here are just a few:

In the 1970s, sociologist Robert Atchley defined as retired a person who collects a pension and is not working full-time. This definition is useful for research studies but may not help us determine our retirement status, given the trend of many working full-time in retirement while collecting a pension.

Retirement also has been defined as an event that occurs when we exit the labor force.[14] This definition leads us to believe that retirement is a single moment in time.

Retirement is referred to as a life stage typically around the age of sixty-two, the age when one can collect partial Social Security benefits. Still there is the question: Are we retired if we collect Social Security benefits and continue working?

Retirement also has been referred to as a "roleless role," a time in life with no particular duties or responsibilities. Does that mean we have no role models that we can emulate?

Some researchers indicate that a person is retired when he or she says so. This definition is inclusive, allowing each person to be a case of one in determining if he or she is retired.

Although these definitions can be confusing, the amorphous concept of retirement has an advantage. The lack of precision and clarity about retirement allows us to create a role that fits our evolving identity and ongoing values. You cannot argue about living the proper or expected retirement life because it doesn't exist.

Retirement and aging are inextricably connected. A fulfilling retirement contributes to healthy aging as it involves satisfaction, intellectual and physical activity and meaningful relationships. How we use this precious gift of time is critical.

WHY NOT USE THE EXISTING (MALE) MODEL OF RETIREMENT?

Traditional (male) retirement planning is based on finances, an emphasis that is critical but not sufficient for women. Relationships, meaning of life and identity are equally important and often overlooked. Women seem open to discussing some of these nonfinancial issues, but few occasions are available to them.[15] New opportunities are needed.

The timing of retirement for women often is different from men's because of women's work history. Women typically have moved in and out of the labor force to care for children while men have experienced a more continuous pattern of employment. Professional women may want to delay their retirement because they entered the workforce later than men and may view retirement as an "imposed interruption" to their work.[16] Also, women often are a few years younger than their partners, which may postpone the timing of their retirement.

Compared to men, women's retirement decisions are generally more influenced by family roles and commitments. More women are care providers, a role and responsibility that often affects their retirement decision.[17] Finally, women tend to prepare for the next life stage differently from men. They talk . . . and are more likely to discuss retirement concerns with ease and honesty.[18] Project Renewment is a retirement and post-career planning process that creates the opportunity for women to discuss nonfinancial and financial issues about their future, reflecting their work histories, roles and communication styles.

PROFESSIONALS AND NONPROFESSIONALS

Do professional and nonprofessional working women have the same concerns and feelings about retirement? According to research conducted by psychologist Christine Price, the answer is no.[19]

Criteria for study participants were that they had to be female, professional or nonprofessional with at least ten years of continuous employment, and retired more than five years. Professional women in her study consisted of educators, university administrators, an editor, gerontologist, anesthesiologist and an IRS customer service representative. Their educational backgrounds ranged from B.S. or B.A. degrees to a Ph.D. and M.D. The nonprofessionals included clerical workers, telephone operators, cafeteria workers, seamstresses and bookkeepers as well as a farmer, factory worker, phone company supervisor and insurance claims processor. Their education ranged from eighth grade to a high school diploma. Although the results are based on a relatively small sample size, Price gives us some insight into the differences.

Attachment to Work: Professional women viewed retirement as an end to a significant chapter in their lives. Some referred to it as a door that is closing on your life, or a time in life when someone pulls the proverbial rug out from under you. They missed their colleagues and clients.[20] Nonprofessionals did not express the same kind of loss. Many were in physically demanding jobs and viewed retirement as a relief and a time to return to more family responsibilities. They were not particularly attached to their employers and many were relieved not to punch a time clock.

Professional Identity: Professional women spoke of losing their identities and having less social status, while nonprofessional women expressed an increase in their sense of importance and responsibility.[21] Despite the loss of identity among professional women, many were able to adapt.

Community Involvement: Although both groups filled their lives with recreational and volunteer opportunities, the types of activities differed between the two groups. Professional retirees engaged in activities related to their careers while the nonprofessionals tended to pursue activities unrelated to their previous employment and occupation.[22]

Although work experiences were different for the two groups, they shared at least three similarities in retirement. Both spent the majority of their time volunteering or taking care of their families. Also, both emphasized the importance of women friends and finally, both showed an ability to adapt to change.[23] Despite these similarities, professionals reported that they had more difficulty adjusting to retirement.

Our hope is to do more than prevent difficult adjustments to retirement. We want the next thirty years or more of career women's lives to be the best possible. This applies to groundbreaking women of the Silent Generation and to the forty million Boomer women who are confronting similar retirement decisions.

Project Renewment has created a process and path that can lead to an exceptional future. It can remove some of the rocks and pebbles from that path, paving the way for younger Boomer career women to Rollerblade into their own period of Renewment.

ABOUT THE BOOK

The book is divided into two sections. The first consists of thirty-eight essays that explore concerns, issues and challenges that might sound familiar to you. From the uncertainty in making a retirement decision to the guilt of reading a novel at 3:00 P.M., we take you through the complexity of the changing lives of career women who either are retired or are contemplating retirement. Some essays may bring a smile to your face; others are more serious. At the end of each essay, there are a few questions and thoughts for you to consider.

The essay section is purposely organized so that you can pick and choose essays that appeal to you. Read whatever strikes your fancy.

The second section is designed to help you create and sustain a Project Renewment group. It consists of guidelines on how to form your own group, the optimum number of participants, topics for discussion, group process and trouble shooting.

A FINAL THOUGHT

John Gardner, in his 1965 commencement speech to graduates from the University of Southern California, addressed the subject of self-renewal and the requirements for it to occur. He said that personal renewal depends on our capacity to remain versatile and adaptive, avoiding being trapped or imprisoned in our routines and comfortable habits. We need to keep "flexibility of the mind, a willingness to listen and learn and an eagerness to try a new way."[24]

He wished the graduates something more difficult than success. He wished them meaning in life. "Meaning is something you build into your life, starting fairly early and working at it fairly hard. You build it out of your own past, out of your affections and loyalties . . . out of the things you believe in . . . and people you love. The ingredients are there. You are the only one who can put them together into that unique pattern that will be your life."[25]

Project Renewment embraces renewal. We hope you are inspired, gain insight and make the best decisions to create an exceptional future. Know that other effective women share your concerns, uncertainties, vision and determination. Enjoy the journey and smile along the way.

Our best wishes to each of you for an extraordinary future of health, fulfillment and joy.

Bernice Bratter　　　Helen Dennis

Part I

Essays

1

RETIREMENT: YES OR NO

If you don't know where you are going,
any road will get you there.

—LEWIS CARROLL

"It was easier to make the decision to divorce my husband than it was to make the decision to retire. I actually thought replacing my husband would be easier than replacing my career," said a sixty-seven-year-old interior designer.

A sixty-six-year-old executive director found that retirement was the hardest decision she ever made. "Work was my life. The people I worked with were my family. Facing my staff and board members to say good-bye was wrenching. I couldn't sleep at night and felt sick. I was saying good-bye to what I had created, to the people who surrounded me and to the biggest part of my life."

Effective women are decisive. We make decisions about policies, products, programs and practices. We negotiate deals, reorganize departments, make hiring and firing decisions and do what it takes to create thoughtful change. Yet, when we are faced with our own decision to retire, many of us wrestle, waffle and even suffer.

Women in Project Renewment shared their views in this back and forth "should I or should I not" retirement conversation they had with themselves.

Here are some of their comments that reflect the allure of retirement: "Retirement means less stress and deadlines." "The alarm clock would be set on 'off' and time would finally belong to me." "Commuting would stop, which means a lot in Los Angeles." "Having the freedom to do what I want to do, when I want to do it." "I will be able to eat better, exercise more and spend more time outdoors." "It's wonderful to know that I will have more of a 'life' to spend with family and friends."

At the same time, they were aware of the downside: "Not working would create a huge void in my life. What would I say when someone asks me 'what do you do?'" "I am afraid of cutting ties with my work, the people, culture and structure." "I would miss the challenge and stimulation."

Personal stories reveal the ambivalence—the pull from and push toward retirement. "It has taken me years to finally make the decision. I thought about all of the reasons to leave my work, but just couldn't do it. I had nothing to go to."

A project manager joined the group at age fifty-nine, eighteen months before she planned to retire. Her company had moved, leaving her with a two-hour commute. "I always assumed that I would work until I was sixty-five, but the long commute is leaving me exhausted. When my family comes over, I can't wait for them to leave. When I am out with friends for a social evening, I can't wait to get home. When my husband talks to me at the end of the day, I have to pretend to listen. I feel as if life is passing me by while I am half asleep. Maybe it's time to retire, but I really don't want to give up my work."

A sixty-seven-year-old woman has been working as an agency director of a nonprofit organization for the past twenty years. "I can never retire. My husband and I never made a financial plan for our future; we also made some unwise investments. It wasn't until I had been at my agency for ten years that the board finally okayed a retirement plan, so I have very little money in my retirement fund. I am sick of managing people and dealing with board members and donors. We do need the money, and I still am working."

A seventy-year-old psychotherapist doesn't know if or when she will retire. "I love my private practice and supervising interns. My husband's health is not good and I need to spend more time with him, although not full-time. I am considering cutting back my hours or eliminating the supervision of interns, but I keep putting it off. If I didn't work, I don't know what I would do with myself. I am not the type of person who is part of the lunch crowd and I really don't have any hobbies. My work is my joy."

Ambivalence is diminished when the retirement decision is determined by internal and external conditions and events. An internal condition is poor health, which nationally is the primary reason for early retirements. External conditions often are imposed by employers who may encourage (legally) early retirement through the elimination of jobs, providing financial incentives and through reorganization. Employers also can make the life of a retirement-eligible employee so miserable that retirement becomes a relief and an escape.

Family and life events affect retirement decisions. A commitment to an ill husband or partner or aging parents can be a compelling force to retire, freeing up time to care for a loved one.

Recent experiences and reactions to work may suggest that retirement is worth considering. Project Renewment women indicated that work may be losing its value if we

- feel exhausted and are unwilling to continue to feel that way;
- are no longer having fun at work;
- feel irritated by colleagues, clients, board members and/or donors;
- are tired of managing people;
- feel out of date;
- sense the employer wants us to leave; and
- no longer feel passionate or challenged by work.

In contrast, our feelings toward work may have the opposite impact, suggesting that retirement may not be the right decision if we

- like starting each day by immersing ourselves in work;
- feel we want to continue to create change within our work environment;
- find work challenging and stimulating;
- feel energized by colleagues;
- enjoy the recognition and appreciation;
- have the energy and capacity to continue; and
- see more opportunities that are exciting and gratifying.

Retiring can be a life-altering experience, especially if we love the challenge, pace and status that work brings to our lives. The decision is more than a financial one. This decision requires us to know ourselves, to be honest about our fears and limits and to be aware of what we need to do to feel alive and vital.

Questions to ask yourself:

1. At this time, how do you feel about your work?
2. How can you envision yourself doing something different?
3. What are your thoughts about part-time work or self-employment?
4. How will your finances influence your retirement decision?
5. Can you identify what you would miss most from your work? How can you experience this in your retirement?

2

I WON'T EARN ANOTHER DOLLAR

*Money is not the only answer, but it makes
a difference.*

— BARACK OBAMA

"It was a stunning moment when I realized it was time to draw
on my retirement funds. I knew I would never earn another dollar. If
any of my investments went south, I would not be able to replace my
losses. It was a frightening and overwhelming feeling, one that I wasn't
prepared for."

This concern came from a successful woman in Project Renewment who had saved and invested significant dollars. And yet, there was something terrifying about the moment she realized "this is it—you are about to live off your retirement savings."

"If only I knew how long I would live," lamented a sixty-year-old architect. "I know I'll be fine if I die before I'm eighty." Perhaps the biggest unknown is how many years are ahead of us. The good news is that we are living longer. The bad news is that our money may not stretch to those bonus years. Stephen M. Pollan and Mark Levine suggest in *Die Broke: A Radical, Four-Part Financial Plan* that the majority of us will not be able to retire in the way that our parents did.[1] The Congressional Budget Office does not agree, suggesting that Boomers' savings behavior is similar to their parents'.[2] Yet only half are saving enough for retirement, assuming they maintain the same standard of living.[3]

Financial planning is critical to establishing economic security in retirement. It is a logical process that requires analysis, projections and strategies, methods that are not new to most of us. As women, we engage in financial planning with an added dimension—our gut feelings about money.

Olivia Mellan, a psychotherapist specializing in problems that involve money, reminds us that women have a history of economic dependency, first on our parents and then, in many cases, on our mates. As competent professionals, most of us want to retain our independence and as a result "tend to have global cataclysmic fear about losing all (our) money and ending up on the street."[4] Mellan believes the root of this fear is based on years of feeling powerless to make enough money to support oneself.

How we think about money is not necessarily rational. Those of us who have accumulated wealth may park and walk ten blocks to avoid paying a parking lot fee. We may shop at thrift stores for our clothing, drive five miles to use a twenty-cent grocery coupon and remain conservative in our expenditures. Those of us with modest incomes may purchase Audis and wear Armani clothing. How we spend doesn't always make sense.

Attitudes play a role in our money behavior. Our parents and early childhood experiences influence how we feel about money. Many of our parents were immigrants who scrimped and saved to buy a home and educate their children. Some lived through the Depression. Many were fiscally conservative because they wanted security and felt a responsibility to leave "something for the children." Their mantras were "Never spend the principal," "Never pay interest" and "Always pay cash."

We absorbed their behaviors and advice. Regardless of the money we accumulate, their mantras still influence some of our decisions and fuel our fears about money. Our parents' warnings are in our heads. The "bag lady syndrome" is a tough image to overcome.

"My parents were impoverished as children and young adults; they lived in fear that they would once again become poor. They passed those fears on to me, even though by the time I was born, my parents were financially comfortable."

The fears persist. "I hang on to old clothing and old things because I am afraid that someday, I will not have the money to buy the new things that I may need, such as clothing and appliances." "I am afraid I will run out of money before I run out of life."

"When I retired, I knew what I had and knew it was not enough. I panicked to the point I felt sick in my stomach. It was clear that I had to figure out ways to get more income. In a few years, I'll probably have to sell my home—which will be very hard."

What are the realities? Poverty and old age are important women's issues. Older women are twice as likely to be poor as men. The annual median income for women 65 and older is about $3,000 above the Census definition of poverty or $11,816.[5] Ninety percent of all women, at some time in their lives, will be totally responsible for their own financial welfare.[6]

We internalize these floating data and statistics, knowing that age and gender are risk factors. This awareness drives our worry. Even though we have income, savings and a retirement plan, the feeling of vulnerability remains. Yes, we are becoming more informed and financially empowered, but many of us feel we aren't where we need to be, just yet.

Being married doesn't change the concern. Although many of us were raised to believe that our husbands would be the ultimate and eternal providers, we know that in many cases, it is not true. Judy Resnick, author of *I've Been Rich. I've Been Poor. Rich Is Better*, tells women that they must take responsibility for their financial security whether or not they are married or have a partner who shares expenses. She writes, "Total dependence on others can be dangerous to your health and your wealth."[7]

Perhaps the fears never disappear. At least we can diminish them by realizing we are in charge of our financial future and if we are willing to take the necessary steps to plan for it.

Questions to ask yourself:

1. What is your attitude toward money? What has influenced your attitude?
2. Do you have a financial plan that you understand?
3. What concrete steps could you take to increase the security of your financial future and increase your comfort level?
4. Do you know how to assess the competency and ethics of financial planners? Do you know how they earn their money from clients?
5. In what ways will retirement affect your lifestyle and will you have the income to support it?

3

CHANGE IS THE NORM

Change is inevitable—except from a vending machine.

—Robert C. Gallagher

Life is moving quickly. We can't believe summer has already disappeared and it's Labor Day. That means Halloween, Thanksgiving and the holidays are close behind. And then it's the New Year. Time is fleeting and seems to "fleet faster" as we age.

Computer systems and the stock market are constantly changing. The weather is unpredictable. Nothing is more permanent than change, but that knowledge offers us little solace.

In our youth, we welcomed change with gusto. At sixteen, we were liberated with a driver's license. Graduations were our launch to the future. Living in a new city was exciting and working in the real world finally happened. Meeting our mate or partner was a dream come true and for many, family life was a blessing. Our careers and life experiences shaped our zest for living. Change was synonymous with expansion, growth and excitement.

And then we turned sixty, or sixty-five, or seventy and realized that change could mean something else. It could mean loss. We may have arthritis, have less retirement income than expected, need to assist our aging parents or have marital problems. We may miss our work and need to move or face living alone.

"After my fall down a flight of stairs, I faced for the first time that my beloved house with its multiple staircases was not age-friendly. My husband's increasing lack of balance and frequent falling exacerbated the situation. As much as I don't want to move, it is clear that I will have to." This was a hard admission for a sixty-five-year-old woman who prided herself on being healthy and fit.

When forced to make decisions because of conditions beyond our control, it is easy to become resentful. Even if we know that losing some energy, stamina and our ability to go into "overdrive" is part of normal aging, that knowledge does not prevent many of us from becoming irritated and frustrated. As a generation of women who have been in control, it is hard to face what has been touted as the "best time of life" when we have to make decisions we would rather not make.

A change caused by poor health is one example of a change we would rather not make. Whether temporary or permanent, these changes are losses. Our women have asked, "How do I deal with the lack of energy caused by chemotherapy?" "How will I take care of myself after my hip replacement surgery?" "Who will care for me after falling so forcefully that my head made a hole in the plaster?" "What will happen if I can no longer drive?" The support of friends and family and their own strength and determination helped these women face and get through such trials, as well as make the difficult decisions for treatment, support and needed services.

Change, on the other hand, has a bright side, according to Project Renewment women.

"Change provides challenges and the chance to learn important lessons, however painful they may be."

"Change alleviates boredom, expands our horizons and provides something new to look forward to. Meeting new people is a big plus."

Retirement was the best change in my life. It allowed me to move from the initial position of "I have to," to the phase of "I need to" and finally to "I want to."

Project Renewment women have adapted. Many found substitutes for what they had left, given up or sacrificed, as volunteers or paid employees. A foundation president became a paid writer, an attorney became a volunteer museum docent and an administrator became a volunteer case manager for a nonprofit family clinic.

A psychotherapist said, "My priorities have changed. I want to travel, pursue recreational activities and do the things I have put off doing."

Avoiding or denying change can affect us both economically and personally. If we anticipate, plan and adapt, we increase our chances of having sufficient retirement income, better health, a higher level of functioning, strong relationships and a purpose. To deny the inevitable changes that accompany later life will only increase our vulnerability and potential for becoming dependent.

In 1967, King Whitney Jr., then president of Personnel Laboratories, is quoted as saying the following in a sales presentation: "Change has a considerable psychological impact on the human mind. To the fearful it is threatening because it means that things may get worse. To the hopeful it is encouraging because things may get better. To the confident it is inspiring because the challenge exists to make things better."[1]

Questions to ask yourself:

1. How have you dealt with change in the past?
2. What attitude and tools will serve you in dealing with changes in your future?
3. Who is the one person you can rely on to support you through a major change?
4. How do you deal with negative change? How do you deal with positive change?
5. What are the changes you can foresee in the future?

WHAT IS PRODUCTIVITY ANYWAY?

*Productivity is being able to do things that you were
never able to do before.*

— FRANZ KAFKA

"If I am not productive, I am irrelevant," said an accomplished
landscape designer.

Being productive is part of our spiritual and psychological core and
for good reason. As career women, we have achieved success by working hard, producing products, strategies, reports, plans, curricula,
experiments, shows and articles. We have increased sales, won court
cases, owned businesses, provided therapy and improved the bottom

line. Promotions, bonuses and kudos have been bestowed upon us for jobs well done. We have sustained successful careers.

Ever since Frederick Taylor introduced the term "productivity" at the turn of the last century, it has been used as a measurement of labor output, efficiency and as a major business determinant. We have responded to this meaning of productivity by fulfilling the demands and expectations of our employers. When these demands disappear, the transition from work to traditional retirement can become a problem. Here is the story of a former attorney in Project Renewment who faced such a situation.

"On a beautiful sunny day, I headed for a local park to read a book written by one of my favorite authors. Reading for pleasure in the middle of a weekday was a new experience for me. Soon after settling in the right spot, I was joined in close proximity by a homeless man who lay back on the grass with his face to the sun. His posture gave every appearance of relaxation and pleasure—and the more comfortable he became the more my discomfort grew. I saw my future as a woman adrift with nothing better to do than sit in the park. I immediately left and made haste for home where no one could see me being lazy and unproductive."

This drive to be productive is within us and doesn't go away simply because we aren't earning a salary anymore. In retirement, there are no performance appraisals or external accountabilities, and no promotions, pay increases or perks. Self-imposed performance reviews based on our career are ineffective.

As highly effective career women of Project Renewment, we struggled to determine what productivity means in later life, post–primary careers. We find that just because we no longer have a real job, the inner switch does not go off. We tell ourselves it is time to savor the pleasures of free time, yet many of us still experience that gnawing sense of guilt, a by-product of not producing.

We derive meaning from the recognition that comes with productivity. Now, for the first time in decades, the measurement of meaningful output cannot be gauged according to a work product. For the first time we are challenged to "let go" of that model. And for many, this is hard.

Old habits don't die easily. A sixty-four-year-old CPA asked, "Why am I rushing from one thing to another? Suppose the task is not done by 11:00 A.M.? Even though I have all week, I still feel that I've just got to finish a task at a certain time and it must be accomplished perfectly. If I don't, I feel that I have failed." Eventually our groups realized that we needed a new definition of productivity, one that reflected new priorities in this post-work phase.

Some of us did indeed experience new meanings for being productive. One Project Renewment member commented, "Productivity now implies accomplishing anything important, making a difference and working to benefit others. It amounts to winding up with new kinds of products and tangible outcomes." These would include painting, acting and photography, producing an opera or even cleaning a closet. Although few of us believed that "closet productivity" had any long-term value.

We identified a shift—from believing that external circumstances must somehow define how productive or useful we are—to defining that value for ourselves. We concluded that this Renewment period is a time to live according to our own values, and be true to ourselves.

Many in our group reported that spending time with their elderly parents or grandchildren was productive. Caring for a sick friend was productive as was time spent walking, doing yoga and Pilates. Keeping healthy was a productive mission and activity.

A therapist commented, "I've graduated (from work), now I even get a massage once a week. I tell myself that's all right to do. It's now okay to focus on me and do fun things; I don't have to be productive twenty-four hours a day. These are new and important values to me."

"I now allow myself to participate in activities that don't have intrinsic value, things that do not necessarily end in the usual kinds of work products. For example, I now spend luxurious periods of time in the sauna at the gym and I take leisurely lunches with friends," commented a speech pathologist.

A market researcher discovered that she didn't care if she never was 100 percent productive again. "Productivity is more about me now and yes, I might need to make some money once in a while, but I'm really starting to redefine what life is about."

"To me the most incredible luxury in my life is waking up and not really knowing what I'm going to do that day and just spontaneously deciding. I don't put anything on my calendar unless it's an appointment, something that is absolutely critical. The rest of it is really all in my head. And I'm very comfortable with just the feeling of doing what I want in this moment." Such were the thoughts of a successful bookseller.

Thanks to the Puritan work ethic, many of us bought into the notion that you only deserved to relax when you died. Despite the culture, most of us have learned to spend some leisure time taking a walk on the beach, having coffee with friends, going to a spa or reading a book. We recognize these are some of the joys of life. We now have guilt-free leisurely days where nourishing our souls is considered productive.

Questions to ask yourself:
1. What does productivity mean to you? Has it changed for you?
2. On a scale of one to five, how important is feeling productive? What makes you feel that way?
3. Write three new "things" you do that make you feel productive.
4. How do you envision a new definition of productivity once you are retired?
5. What, if anything, do you believe entitles you to be less productive (in the traditional sense) than you were in your career?

5

I ONLY CRY AT THE MOVIES

Crying opens the lungs, washes the countenance, exercises the eyes and softens down the temper. So cry away.

—MR. BUMBLE IN CHARLES DICKENS'S *Oliver Twist*

Crying is good for us. It relieves stress, rids our body of toxins and makes us feel better. It is considered natural, healthy and curative.[1] Although rarely mentioned in the psychiatric literature, crying is considered the most natural way to cope with pain, tension and sorrow.[2]

And yet for some of us, crying is difficult. One of our Project Renewment women spoke with despair about the deterioration of her last living relative, whom she adored. She was so upset she wanted to cry, but couldn't except in the darkness of a movie theater. Surprisingly this inability to cry is shared by high-achieving women in our groups.

"During my husband's illness, I could not cry at home and certainly not at work. Finally I was able to cry in two places: while driving in the privacy of my car and in my yoga class," said a nonprofit CEO.

Growing up, many of us were told, "Big girls don't cry." And we all wanted to be big girls. We were told as young mothers, "Never cry in front of your children. It might upset them." And we did not want to upset the children. The message that "it's not okay to cry" followed many women throughout their lives.

Crying is a reactive form of communication that conveys how we are feeling. In the workplace we are expected to communicate verbally and quickly learn how to control an outward expression of anger, sadness or frustration. And God forbid we should cry in front of men. We would be mortified of losing our power. Outwardly emotional women are sometimes perceived as hysterical and unstable, so we keep our tears locked up only to discover that when we are ready for the release, we cannot cry.

The only high-ranking woman in a distribution company lost credibility with her male peers when she cried in an executive meeting. A male member of the group gruffly and disrespectfully criticized one of her assumptions. She lost control and cried. The news spread throughout the company and the woman never regained the respect from her peers.

In Ancient Greece and the Middle Ages, public crying was normal. The Greek warrior Odysseus cries in almost every chapter of Homer's *Iliad* and St. Francis of Assisi was said to have been blinded by weeping.[3] In the sixteenth century, crying and sobbing at a play, opera or symphony was considered fitting for both men and women. Tears were a sign of sensitivity.[4]

The Industrial Revolution stopped the public flow of tears. Workers needed to be diligent rather than overtly emotional. And children were taught that the act of crying was the real problem, rather than the reaction to the problem.[5] As the public became uncomfortable with a public display of tears, leaders no longer cried in public. In 1972, tears worked against the late senator Edmund Muskie's presidential campaign as he defended his wife against a scurrilous and untrue attack.[6] The senator was perceived as being out of control. Tearless generations have followed.

Women in several groups remarked, "I can't cry. Instead, I get a stomachache, clench my fists and get angry." "I feel ashamed when I become overly emotional. I see it as losing control."

Times may be changing. "In just a few short decades, we've gone from the view that crying is just a loss of control and a sign of weakness to a common perception that there might be some value in open emotional crying."[7] Public figures are weeping without shame. Gywneth Paltrow cried so hard on national television when she received the Oscar for best actress, she barely could talk. Former senator Bob Dole became tearful when he remembered the people in his home state that came to his assistance when he suffered war injuries. And President Bill Clinton has been teary-eyed on a regular basis.[8]

Public crying is becoming more accepted and may be considered an asset, particularly among politicians who want to share the sensitive side of their lives. Essayist Anne Taylor Fleming notes that "the only politicians who cannot cry in America are women."[9] After Pat Schroeder withdrew from the 1988 presidential race she was criticized and even hounded for shedding tears in public.[10]

Research has been conducted on crying and tears. Emotional tears have been found to be chemically different from tears shed when peeling an onion. They contain more of the body's natural pain relievers— beta-endorphins. And emotional tears have more toxins than tears from pollution and eye irritation. The relief we feel from crying may be due to the removal of toxins accumulated during periods of stress[11] and therefore increase our body's ability to heal itself.[12] Scientists are concluding that people who are able to cry for emotional reasons may have better emotional and physical health than those who cannot.[13]

Poets and novelists must have known that crying was good for us. Shakespeare wrote: "To weep is to make less the depth of grief."[14]

And Tennyson wrote about a woman whose husband was killed at war: "She must weep or she will die." On a lighter note, the exquisite Sophia Loren reminds us that "If you haven't cried, your eyes can't be beautiful."[15]

"Tears reflect a profound humanity."[16] According to William Frey, a biochemist and tear expert, humans are the only animals that cry because of emotions. In the Renewment phase of life, tears from fear, sadness or stresses demonstrate not only our humanity, but our ability to be authentic without repercussions.

Questions to ask yourself:

1. How do you feel about crying?
2. When was the last time you cried? Were there any repercussions?
3. What makes you cry?
4. What did you learn about crying while growing up? What did you learn about crying while on the job?
5. How would you like to modify any expression of your emotions?

6

WHO AM I WITHOUT A BUSINESS CARD?

The value of identity . . . is that so often it comes with purpose.

—RICHARD R. GRANT

Our business card is gone. Without it, we feel naked. Giving up that rectangle-shaped piece of card stock is like giving up part of ourselves. So often we have been asked, "May I have your card?" And how many times have we handed over our card, collected one in return and then added the new one to the stack on our desk?

We have used business cards to network, develop new business and make an impression. We keep them in our purses, briefcases, wallets and desks. We store them in attractive cases so they don't get bent; we include them in our correspondence. We write something clever on the back to give people a reason to hold on to them.[1] We use them to introduce ourselves to prospects we may meet at cocktail parties, conferences or the theater.

The business card is important. It not only tells others how to contact us, but tells them what we do and who we are—an attorney, psychologist, vice president, manager, director and more. With a card, we don't have to explain ourselves.

The use of business and visiting cards began in the seventeenth century with the French, Chinese and Germans all claiming responsibility for this invention. Business cards were used in the United States in the nineteenth century to promote an individual's business,[2] not their identity.

A former executive director of a large nonprofit organization tells her story.

"My first trip to a department store after retirement was on a weekday afternoon. It felt strange since I never went shopping during the week in daylight hours. My quest was to buy a new lipstick. I wandered over to the cosmetic counter, where I ran into a former member of my board of directors. I had hoped that I would not bump into anyone, let alone a person who had only known me in my professional capacity. If only I could have told her that I was on a mission for a famous visiting dignitary who realized she was without a lipstick. Then it happened. 'How is retirement?' she asked. 'I am not retired,' I snarled. You might have thought she had asked me, 'How do you like your new career as a topless dancer?' 'I am doing some consulting,' I informed her. 'Do you have a card?' she asked. I didn't and even though I was consulting, I didn't feel like I had a real job, particularly without a card."

While career women are still in the workforce, they typically do not suffer from identity crises. Such crises have been associated with adolescents and midlife men, not with well-established professional women. Yet identities can and do become fragile when the career disappears.

Two months into retirement, a woman was asked the dreaded retirement question at the grocery store. "What do you do?" Her reply: "I used to be a stockbroker." She couldn't bring herself to say, "I'm retired." It made her feel invisible. She told women in her Project Renewment group, "Unfortunately, I didn't have the forethought to have had a card made to reveal my retirement identity."

Women have made great progress. Shortly after Madeleine Albright was sworn in as secretary of state, Henry Kissinger introduced her to an audience by formally welcoming her into the "fraternity" of those who had held that position. Replying, she said, "Henry I hate to tell you, but it's not a fraternity anymore."[3]

As card-carrying effective women, we make many career positions gender neutral. We have influenced and been witness to more women in colleges, medical schools, law schools and on Wall Street than ever before. Given our pioneering efforts, we are troubled by the idea that we may lose that influence once we lose our professional cards and their direct link to identities that make us so proud.

If business cards are important to us in retirement, we can create new and clever ones. A retired news reporter uses a card that says, "Executive in Charge of Everything." A retired executive took a different approach; she uses a golf tee that has her name engraved on it. A retired lawyer used an orange card with three boxes: art director, lawyer and used-car salesperson. A check mark is placed next to art director. Just because we are retired does not mean that people won't want to contact us.

A card is not only a card, but more. It has become a standard way to introduce ourselves, market our products and services and identify who we are in our professional lives and in our retirement lives. Our challenge is to create an identity—with or without a card—that continues to have personal value and meaning.

Questions to ask yourself:

1. When did you get your first business card? How did it make you feel?
2. How would you feel without a business card?
3. If you were to create a business card that reflects who you are or what you believe in, what would it say?
4. What would be your elevator speech if someone asks you what you do?
5. How would you like to handle the business-card culture in your retirement?

7

ADDICTED TO POWER

Every form of addiction is bad.

—Carl Gustav Jung

"I am a stimulation junkie—an excitement addict. When I am standing in front of a group of people who are feverishly writing down my every word, I am on a high. I like being in the limelight. The adulation, recognition and applause thrill me. Nothing has ever made me feel more important. I can't imagine life without it. I fear being bored and boring." So speaks a Project Renewment woman who has given speeches around the world.

The director of a corporate foundation says, "When I think about the challenges I have from my work, I feel a fire in my belly. I shudder when I think about retirement because I have had to give up too much to get to where I am. I like the perks of my job. On the other hand, I have sacrificed a lot. I need to look at what I have missed along the way."

And another likes being special: "I have no desire to be an ordinary person."

An international business consultant finds that her job feeds into her desire for recognition. "When I am doing everything right and getting feedback and validation, I feel great about myself. I thrive on being driven around in limousines and flown on private planes. The adrenaline rush of closing an important deal throws me over the top. I love the power. And I like the treatment I get because I am powerful. I also, however, am exhausted and my marriage is going through another agonizing transition. Am I missing out on too many of life's simple pleasures?"

These women worked hard to be accomplished, effective and recognized. They have competed with men and missed the time to be with their families. With ambivalence they are taking stock of their achievements and the price they paid. Longtime work habits are hard to break. As we give up the starring role and step down from the stage, the withdrawal can be palpable and frightening.

"When I was working I became another person. As a political fundraiser, I was aggressive, fearless and successful. I found my way into places and with people not ordinarily available to others. I never thought of power as an addiction, but I sure missed it when I retired. Suddenly, people were not taking my calls and invitations to high-level events were no longer automatic. I felt as if I was in shock, but I didn't have any shock absorbers."

Another woman told us her ex-husband is an alcoholic. "I attended Al-Anon and could easily see his addiction. I was unaware of my own until I realized that I continued working even when my body was telling me that I was breaking down. The reason was that I wanted to be successful. I couldn't let go of being exceptional in the eyes of others even though it made me sick."

Addiction is an "uncontrollable compulsion to repeat a behavior regardless of its consequences."[1] Although it is most often used in conjunction with alcohol or drugs, addiction also applies to work. Pursuing power, praise and excitement with no regard to its impact could be detrimental to our well-being. By ignoring the consequences, we may risk damage to our health, marriage and other relationships. Indeed, we may be addicts. If this is the case, there is help. Based on the principles of Alcoholics Anonymous, Workaholics Anonymous was established in 1983 to help individuals who want to stop working compulsively.[2] A good therapist can also help.

As with any addiction, stopping "cold turkey" causes serious withdrawal. Leaving a career often is highly emotional and agonizingly intense. Our addiction is not sold at the street corner and is not illegal. In fact, it is part of the Puritan ethic.

"I teach project management to engineers and managers anywhere from a one-hour lecture to five full days at a time. I always get a fantastic response from the attendees. My sense of worth is in direct response to the adulation, and I am addicted to that. If I do not teach for a month and get my fix, I doubt my value. I need that fix to feel good about myself. The question is, 'Can I give it up?' 'What can I do that will be just as self-validating?' 'How can I let go and still feel whole?'"

Letting go is a challenge. Our past can serve us well for our future. The qualities that will keep us intact are those that made us successful in our careers—drive, ability, discipline, commitment, determination and vision, to name a few. Perhaps the biggest change is the source from which we derive value. The shift from a full-time highly charged career to "whatever is next" suggests that we may have to diminish our need for external validation and place equal or greater value on internal validation, the feeling of value that comes from within.

This transition may not be easy. At some point, the consequences of work addiction become apparent. It becomes more difficult to be on call 24/7, and the sleepless nights and stressful meetings become debilitating. The long hours and travel take a toll. The marriage becomes shaky. The grandchildren are rarely seen. These consequences are drivers for change.

Life is finite and eventually we realize that time is a gift. As we examine our lives, choices become more apparent and the impact of withdrawal diminishes. If we believe that the most powerful and gratifying position is to know who we are, what is important and feel good about ourselves, we will be free of our addiction and open to renewal.

Questions to ask yourself:

1. How much praise, power and excitement do you need in your life?
2. Where do you get your validation?
3. What outside of your work is meaningful and motivating?
4. How well do you know yourself?
5. How can you add more fulfillment to your life?

8

LESS STEAM IN MY ENGINE

America's number one energy crisis is
Monday morning.

—Unknown

"I mourn the superwoman I used to be," is a common lament of effective career women who feel their engines losing a bit of steam. The feeling of diminished energy is high on the list of grievances for women who at one time had the energy of two or three people. Getting tired is looked upon as not living up to expectations or, worse yet, failing.

At one time, those of us who considered ourselves superwomen had endless energy. We did everything. We were successful in our jobs, took work home to prepare for meetings, nurtured our children, applied Band-Aids to scraped knees, went to soccer games, attended children's piano lessons, entertained our husband's clients, never perspired and only rarely fell asleep during the adagio movement at a concert. Our standards were high because we did everything well—all of the time.

It is common for career women to say, "Why am I so tired after flying across the country?" "Why am I zapped the morning after I work late?" "Why do I want to nap at 3:00 P.M.?" We can find reasons for occasional fatigue. The reality is we might be tired because we behaved as though we are three people. The other part of the reality is that we are aging.

The risk in discussing this issue is that it plays into stereotypes about getting older, particularly in the workplace. Energy is associated with youth, not older age. Some employers have crossed the line of age discrimination by saying that "we are looking for a younger, more energetic person." Nonprofit organizations are not exempt from this type of sentiment. A president of a "do good" nonprofit organization was heard saying, "We need a young, energetic chair of our membership committee who will get the job done."[1]

The loss of vigor can be difficult to face and accept for several reasons. First, we may not be able to do everything we want to do. Second, we may feel others perceive our slowing down as becoming "old," triggering stereotypes associated with age. Third, we may feel powerless if our lack of energy is related to physical health, such as chronic conditions of heart disease or arthritis, or from the side effects of chemotherapy or radiation treatments.

One way to enhance energy levels is to maintain our strength. As part of the normal aging process, we lose muscle mass. If we don't exercise, that loss translates into weakness, requiring more energy to walk, lift and just move. The good news is that weight resistance exercises build muscle tissue at any age, which in turn, enhances our vigor.

Not everyone loses energy at the same rate, the same amount or at the same age. Each person is unique. With training, some may lose very little energy and strength. We all know seventy-five-year-old hikers, bikers and runners. An eighty-seven-year-old woman ran the 2007 New York Marathon. Four percent of the runners in that marathon (almost 1,500 of the 37,000) were over sixty years old.[2] Their training paid off.

Einstein said that insanity is "doing the same things over and over again and expecting different results."[3] How many times do we over-book commitments and wonder why we are tired? How many trips do we need to take before realizing that the morning after we return from another time zone, we will feel fatigued? How many times does it take for us to know that after throwing a big dinner party, we may need to stay in bed the next morning? Why are we always surprised? The consistent belief that we will always have that overdrive suggests we may be slightly deranged and occasionally delusional.

A sixty-three-year-old CEO of a nonprofit talked about her experience. "I was recognized as being tireless in surpassing my goals for my organization. Now I grow tired and I wonder who I have become."

She went on to say, "I used to be able to function well on four to five hours of sleep each night. Now, I need a good seven to eight hours to feel rested. I miss having those extra hours in the morning and feel as if I lost part of my day."

We are a generation of women used to thriving on overdrive. There was always that extra bit of energy to get it done, whatever it was. We had a reserve tank. It seems that the tank has become slightly depleted with age. We still can exert ourselves with determination and shift into high gear to get the job done—but sometimes at a price. That price is temporary fatigue.

There is a flip side to this issue. Bernard Baruch tells us that "Experience achieves more with less energy and time."[4] Rather than doing it all, we now can focus on the riches that a lifetime of experience makes clear to us. Having less energy requires us to prioritize, to think about how we expend time, to consider what we want to do and the relative importance of our activities. During our earlier years, we approached our commitments horizontally, with many activities ranking number one at the same time. Today, we can take a vertical approach, much like climbing a mountain. The most important activity should be on top.

We confront and deal with life, each in our own time. Although a little delusion never hurts, a lifetime of belief that we always will have the energy of a twenty-year-old can lead to disappointment and frustration. Review, prioritize and select what is most important. Only then do we have the greatest chance to live a life of personal meaning and value.

Questions to ask yourself:

1. If you have lost energy, how is that manifested?
2. How do you compensate for changes in energy?
3. How do you retain your vitality?
4. What does loss of vigor mean to you?
5. What can you do to maintain energy and vigor, but don't?

9

WORK *AND* RETIREMENT?

Retirement: World's longest coffee break . . .

— UNKNOWN

The working retired may sound like an oxymoron, but not today. One of the most profound changes in the American institution of retirement is the inclusion of work. The reasons are many. Economics is a major driver. But dollars and cents are only part of the story. Our attitudes, family history and aspirations influence our feelings about money and the decisions we make.

Although men and women pursue retirement careers for income, they also work to stay mentally and physically active, remain productive and useful,[1] and to be part of something larger than themselves. Some work for health benefits[2] while others want to explore a new field or pursue dreams. Work has always been part of our American culture and value system. It is what we do.

There is little research about reasons career women in particular return to work. Sigmund Freud gave us a clue: "Love and work are the cornerstones of our humanness."[3] Work has been (or is) a cornerstone for all Project Renewment women. If we accept Freud's view, what happens to our humanness if we no longer work?

For many of our retired Project Renewment women, work remains seductive. One woman who was adamant about cherishing her freedom took on a consulting project. Other women declared themselves retired, that is, unless they were approached for a freelancing assignment. Just seeing the opportunity to work lured many women, not as employees, but as self-employed professionals.

This was true for an executive vice president for public affairs at a large utility company. At forty-nine she retired, took a year's sabbatical and then started her own human resource/coaching firm in another state. In another instance a private sector documentary filmmaker switched to making videos for nonprofits. Both a former ombudsman and a nonprofit executive used their hobbies of adventure-travel and photography to produce works of fine art. They have exhibited their photos, sold them and created greeting cards. A program manager returned to work as a paid book-group leader with requests for more groups than she could possibly handle. All of these women used retirement as a time to awaken or reawaken their lifelong passions. All are self-employed.

Some of our women retired and then changed their minds. One said, "Retirement is not for me. I can't take it. I have been continuously sick since I retired and that is not like me. I have to go back to work to regain my health." She is actively seeking part-time employment.

Societal norms have dictated a sequence of work followed by retirement. The pattern was simple, predictable and made sense since many workers were exhausted from their jobs and looked forward to a time of rest and relaxation for the remainder of their years. Regardless of the roles, work was for money; in retirement, it was not.

Our parents' generation of retirees exemplified the traditional model of retirement. "My seventy-five-year-old retired father built a park to honor a fallen leader. My retired mother was the treasurer of several nonprofit organizations that used her accounting skills. As retirees, neither thought that their type of retirement activities should be for pay. Fortunately they did not need the money."

Although many of us love our careers and may be reluctant to leave them, we also are drawn to the new freedom of retirement. Others are eager to leave their work but cannot afford to retire. This push and pull of ambivalent feelings is not unusual.

Does it make sense to retire and then work? For some, yes. If we're lucky, we can determine when we are going to retire and for what reasons. Some employers are responding to midlife and older persons' desire and need to continue working by offering phased retirement and job sharing programs. Both retain valuable talent while easing employees' transition to retirement.

Federal policies are working in our favor. In 1978, Congress raised the mandatory retirement age from the traditional sixty-five to seventy. Eight years later, in 1986, the mandatory retirement age was removed for most jobs, meaning that employees could not be automatically retired because of their age. Exceptions are fashion models, firefighters, police, airline pilots, bus drivers, air traffic controllers, executives receiving more than $44,000 from a company pension and members of the United States Diplomatic Corps/Foreign Service.[4] One would think that a seasoned and experienced diplomat would be highly valued.

Federal law also protects against age discrimination in the workplace for employees forty years old and over. According to the Age Discrimination in Employment Act (ADEA), it is unlawful for employers with twenty or more employees to discriminate in employment, termination, compensation, training and benefits. Age discrimination is difficult to prove and, although illegal, is still pervasive.

If we love our work and our careers, we can still stay involved, make a contribution and earn a few dollars too. We may pursue opportunities to stay with our current employer part-time or change employers. We also can change our minds and move from full retirement back to employment. Taking off time for a sabbatical, experimenting with a variety of learning opportunities and trying something new are all available to us. Given the competitive work environment, we still need to stay current on the knowledge, skills and practices of the day to remain employable.

Yes, work does make sense during retirement, if that is what we want or need to do for purse or for soul.

Questions to ask yourself:

1. When will you be ready to leave your career?
2. What are your strengths and how do you want to continue to use them?
3. If you are considering work during retirement, what are the "goodies" or benefits you want that will make each day a terrific one?
4. How can you identify work opportunities for collaborating with a colleague that will enable you to do what you enjoy?
5. What new kinds of work would you like to pursue?

10

FEELING VULNERABLE

To be human is to be vulnerable—this I must accept.

—Obi

"The first time I was in touch with my vulnerability was when I broke my shoulder while skiing. This accident was a turning point. Even though healthy and fit, I now realize that I am older and even I can get hurt. It was a rude awakening."

An interior designer decided to go ice skating with her grandson. "I hadn't been on ice skates since I was a teenager. Right off the bat I fell and broke my wrist. How crazy I was to think that I am still a kid."

Our physical vulnerabilities are not obvious. There is no alarm bell that rings before we pick up our forty-five-pound grandson or push the heavy trash can to the curb for pickup. There are few signs that warn us to ski less dangerous slopes, warm up before ice skating or avoid standing on the highest step of a ladder. Since chronological age is a poor predictor of any performance, it's hard to know when to reduce, avoid or stop certain physical activities. Often it's a pulled muscle or broken bone that serves as a reminder.

Physical risks in our home environment are easier to assess and avoid. Most accidents among older adults occur in the home, and often in the bathroom. Here is one story where that knowledge is put to use. "As a new widow, I found myself living alone after a forty-year marriage. I was always busy, so busy that I felt placing a mat in the tub took too much time. It wasn't important until I had an epiphany. If I fell and couldn't get up, who would know? The thought was frightening enough that I have become a bathtub mat advocate and user."

We all need reminders to minimize accident risks at home — remove loose throw rugs, install bathroom bars, keep hallways uncluttered and have proper lighting, just to name a few. For whatever reason, we are often slow to apply household safety to our own lives. Perhaps it's our resistance to acknowledge that age does affect our reaction time, flexibility and speed, even if we are fit. The challenge is to realize that home accident prevention is not just the subject of research reports or news articles, but relevant to our safety and well-being.

Vulnerability is also highly personal. "Never let them see you sweat" and "never show your weaknesses" are mantras of perceived strength and leadership. As highly effective women, many of us had to be strong and resilient throughout our careers. In this stage of our lives, there may be times when we are not at our prime because of poor health, depression, family responsibilities, spousal conflict or financial problems. When we are not at our best, it is easy to feel vulnerable.

In some cases, we inadvertently create our own problem. Many of us have established a self-image as competent strong women with a self-imposed standard of infinite excellence. The image is so strong that there is little room to falter. As we move from work to retirement and from youth to older age, there are bound to be bumps in the road, sometimes even moguls (for the skiers) that will make us feel vulnerable. The events are beyond our control and part of the life course.

When we are vulnerable we have no choice but to be genuine. We learn to accept who we are. As we strive to become more authentic, we may be more open for others to see us as we really are, exposing our flaws and shortcomings. The more authentic we become, the higher the risk that we will reveal something personal, awkward or even embarrassing to ourselves and others.

We asked working and retired women in Renewment groups, "What makes you feel vulnerable?" Here are some answers to the statement "I feel vulnerable when I":

- am aware of my financial limitations and downsizing possibilities;
- am criticized by anyone, even when I ask for it;
- celebrate milestone birthdays;
- have unresolved problems with my children and grandchildren;
- realize I don't have adult children to turn to when things might be tough;
- am judged by my spouse, partner or significant other;
- have hurt someone else;
- know my life is compromised by chronic health problems;
- feel rejected by friends;
- acknowledge that it is a fight to stay healthy;
- drive in heavy traffic and fear "crazy drivers;" and
- read about global threats in the world news.

Some women commented that exposing shortcomings to children was particularly difficult. Regardless of our age or the age of our children, we want to protect them. Several women indicated how hard it was to discuss end-of-life concerns with their adult children. Perhaps death is perceived as the ultimate vulnerability.

What is the antidote? One is confidence. The more confident the women were about their finances, health, abilities and self-worth, the less they felt at risk or concerned. And yet being overconfident may mask our ability to deal with real risks.

The second is control. The women agreed that feeling in control lessened their concerns and fears. Yet we know that we never have total control. The best we can do is to use our knowledge and good judgment to exert as much influence as possible to minimize risks to our body, soul and spirit.

Oprah Winfrey says she allows herself to be vulnerable. "It's not something I do consciously. But I am. It just happens that way."[1] Our approach to vulnerability is to minimize risks that could compromise us physically and emotionally, and accept what cannot be changed and learn from it. Yet one could argue that being vulnerable means being intellectually and emotionally open to new experiences. And perhaps that is what Oprah meant. To be alive is to be vulnerable.

Confidence as an antidote is important but limited, and control is what we strive for but never can totally achieve. Perhaps we need to reframe vulnerability, accepting what we cannot change and making the most of it. Acknowledging our vulnerability may make us become more aware of our need for others and also increase our sensitivities to the needs of others. Part of the wisdom we gain as we get older is living in the face of this new vulnerability.

Questions to ask yourself:
1. What makes you feel vulnerable? Make a list.
2. What are your feelings about vulnerability?
3. How do you react to others when you feel vulnerable?
4. How does it affect your relationships?
5. Have there been repercussions as a result of your vulnerability?

11

ANTIAGING OR PRO-AGING

Everything has beauty, but not everyone sees it.

—Confucius

"The term 'antiaging' is negative, inappropriate and offensive to me," says a gerontologist.

We have been destined to fight aging every step of the way. The theme is centuries old. Ponce de León searched for the Fountain of Youth in the late 1400s. Medieval writers told of Alexander the Great searching for such waters in eastern Asia. The Polynesians had a similar fable that located the Fountain of Youth in Hawaii.[1]

Americans continue to search for the miracle, providing a large market for the antiaging industry that includes foods, nutritional supplements, age-defying hair products, remedies for sexual dysfunction, memory improvement, cosmetic surgery and "cosmaceuticals," a combination of cosmetics and pharmaceuticals. There are 1,700 nonprescription lotions, creams and gels that promise dramatic results for aging skin. Boomers, unwilling to give up their youth, are pouring $30 billion a year into antiaging products.[2] This is the generation that repeatedly said, "Never trust anyone over thirty."

From an interior designer we heard, "The antiaging stuff fills me with revulsion. It's like living in a bubble from the fountain of youth. I am surrounded by the marketing of looking young."

Not everyone has bought into Botox. A teacher said, "I don't like the hanging flesh on my arms or the wrinkles around my mouth, but I wouldn't do anything about it."

Society sends us strong messages about aging. In the work environment, looking older typically is not considered a plus, particularly with younger competitors, supervisors and interviewers. "In the nineties, a youthful look became a business accessory. Today it is a necessity."[3] Cosmetic companies tell us to buy makeup that will defy our age. Film, television and advertising have paid little attention to age,[4] even though almost one out of eight Americans is sixty-five years or older. And retailers are just beginning to realize that the figure of a sixty-year-old woman is just a little different from that of a twenty-year-old.

The largest organization that has placed aging on the enemy list is the American Academy of Anti-Aging Medicine. Established in 1993 by Dr. Ronald Klatz, it has a membership of 11,500 physicians, health practitioners and scientists in sixty-five countries. There are more physicians in the academy than geriatricians in the entire United States. The academy has published five medical textbooks on antiaging medicine, continues to mail more than one million pieces of educational material annually to physicians, scientists, the media and members of Congress, conducted seventeen international conferences and provided continuing education for thousands of physicians and surgeons.[5] The Academy defines antiaging as a medical specialty that not only stops aging, but reverses it.

Not everyone agrees. Gerontology researchers S. Jan Olshansky, Leonard Hayflick and Bruce A. Carnes stated in a 2002 *Scientific American*[6] article that "No current marketed intervention—none—has yet proved to slow, stop or reverse human aging,"[7] a statement endorsed by fifty-one internationally recognized investigators.

The two warring factions debate one another point by point on subjects such as hormones and organ replacements. The gerontology researchers say no hormone has been proven to slow, stop or reverse aging. They do, however, acknowledge experiments where short-term use of hormones has had a favorable impact on muscle and skin elasticity. The antiaging group quotes a study from a 1990 edition of the *New England Journal of Medicine* that found using human growth hormones does indeed increase muscle mass, an indicator of aging reversal.

The gerontology researchers say replacing body parts with youthful ones to increase longevity is a possible theory, but highly improbable. The antiaging group states that replacement parts for worn-out or damaged human organs have already helped people live longer and increase their healthy life span.

Some antiaging advocates believe that advances in the field are paving the way to "practical immortality" with human life reaching to 150 years. Gerontology researchers do not deny that we may increase life expectancy. They generally agree that life expectancy may be increased by reducing calories while maintaining adequate nutrition. Since most of the caloric restriction research, however, has been conducted with animals, they are uncertain about the effects of caloric restriction on humans.

Martha Holstein, a researcher at the Parkridge Center for the Study of Health, Faith, and Ethics in Chicago, writes that antiaging sends a bad message to women. It forces them to try to be forever youthful, implying that being and looking your age is not good.[8]

Some women resist changing nature for the purpose of looking young. "I would never risk surgery for anything other than my health."

In her book *Time of Your Life,* Jane Glenn Haas discussed her face-lift. She never thought she would have one, thinking she would rather spend her money by traveling to Egypt. Well, at sixty she went to Egypt, "looking tired and old."[9] Breast cancer meant no more hormone replacement therapy. And without artificial estrogen, "fat pads rearranged themselves." "Newton's law of gravity took over."[10] Subsequently, she decided to spend part of an inheritance to "tamper with God's handiwork." As a result, she feels more confident, visible again and renewed. "[It's] like having naturally curly hair that is a part of me that I don't have to fuss with anymore to feel presentable."[11]

Another Project Renewment woman changed her mind about an antiaging procedure. "I tried human growth hormone injections for six months and didn't see any major changes. In fact, I realize that growth hormones can be dangerous and can encourage the growth of remote cancer cells. I now support prevention of premature aging rather than repair."

There is a distinction between looking younger and looking better. A gerontologist in Project Renewment was interviewed by a television anchor on the topic of staying young. She was asked what changes she made as she got older. In addition to increased exercise and better nutrition, she mentioned she colored her hair. "Aha," said the interviewer. That means you support antiaging measures. The gerontologist replied, "Not necessarily, it just means that my hair is mousy gray and quite unattractive. Looking good is not an indication of antiaging."

The cosmetic industry is slowly getting the message that female Boomers are a proud generation that doesn't want to feel ashamed about getting older. In 2007, Dove launched an ad campaign for a new product line of soap and lotions branded "pro.age." One of their ads showed an older nude woman with a tagline of "Too old to be in an antiaging ad . . . but this isn't antiage. This is pro.age." Dove ads say they are "celebrating women over 50." Given that the fifty-plus market has discretionary income and spends, Dove's product line and marketing strategy are smart, on target and potentially good business.

"The secret of staying young is to live honestly, eat slowly and lie about your age," stated Lucille Ball. Although we have not discovered the secrets of youth, her comment makes us chuckle. If staying young, however, means looking like we did thirty years ago, cosmetic surgery is the solution and not a secret.

An alternative and more achievable goal to staying young is to look and be the best we can be. We create our own beauty with healthy nutrition, exercise, managing stress, continuing curiosity, constantly learning and doing what we love to do. Being an authentic person is beautiful.

Questions to ask yourself:

1. How do you feel about the antiaging movement?
2. Are you engaging in antiaging activities or using products that might place you at risk? If yes, what are they?
3. What are you doing to slow the aging process—naturally?
4. How do you feel about beauty as you age?
5. Can you envision a new personal idea of what is a beautiful woman?

12

IS BUSY BETTER?

It is not enough to be busy. So are the ants.
The question is: What are we busy about?

—HENRY DAVID THOREAU

Imagine the feeling of euphoria during the first month of retirement. There are no deadlines, e-mails, commutes, office politics or pressures. The time is ours, yet we still haven't slowed down. Our calendars are filled with so much to do that we can hardly catch our breath. This initial period of retirement is often referred to as the honeymoon phase.[1] Many of us will feel exhilarated—at least for a while. So began the experience of one newly retired woman in Project Renewment.

"In the first few months of my retirement I was so busy I didn't know how I ever had time to work. The first thing I did was to take everything that was broken out of my storage cupboard and have it repaired. That included the vacuum, cracked porcelain plate and the bent silver spoon. I cleaned and organized my house. I took clothes to the tailors, shoes to the shoemaker and I had the house painted and windows washed. I even tackled the garage. I went on a trip to India and had breakfasts, lunches and dinners with old friends. I took yoga classes and long walks in the middle of the day. I read books and took computer lessons, honing my skills since I no longer had an assistant. My biggest luxury was reading the morning newspaper—in the morning.

"After everything got fixed and I grew tired of eating at restaurants every day, life began to feel superficial. I panicked when I realized that I was busy—and bored. I didn't miss work, but I missed the mental stimulation, camaraderie and challenges that I had while working. I was scared that I could never find these things again in retirement."

Clearly something was missing.

The early days of retirement are filled with choices: a time to catch up with friends, take the extra yoga and Pilates classes and start (and complete) the never-ending to-do lists. There is even a choice to do nothing. We initially may feel liberated and relieved, knowing we now have the time to do all of those things for which there was no time during our working years. This glorious honeymoon can last a lifetime or disappear and reappear many times.

At one time, retirement was considered the most stable period of life; today it can be one of the most dynamic life stages. And change is an integral part of it. Since retirement is an opportunity that can last as long as thirty years, just being busy for that amount of time may not be sufficient.

One of the unsettling retirement experiences of successful women is the prospect of an empty calendar. We are used to filling every minute, knowing where we are supposed to be, what projects are due and what clients to meet. Now the calendar is empty. If not, it is filled with different kinds of appointments—the doctor, mechanic, hairstylist and trainer. One woman commented, "Sometimes I write my own name on my calendar so I think I'm busy.

"There's part of me that finds the prospect of not having something to do all day—every day a delicious concept. And then there's part of me that is panicky about the idea that I'm not going to have something to do every day, that I am going to get bored, lose my sense of self-worth and not have anything to talk about to people."

Why do we feel so compelled to be busy? Part of the answer is the Puritan work ethic. The Puritans were members of a group of English Protestants in the seventeenth century who were advocates of strict religious discipline. Their teachings were based on their Bible and emphasized hard work and perfection as necessary for salvation.[2] Pleasure was considered sinful.[3] Puritanism was well received by early capitalists because it created a self-disciplined and hardworking labor force. These values continue to define the American work ethic. American employees often do not take the full amount of paid vacation time because of the stress of returning to work to face a slew of e-mails and a huge to-do list. They also fear their absence will affect their job security. One-quarter of Americans don't have any paid vacation time, and those who do have fourteen days; the French have thirty-nine days and the Brits twenty-four.[4]

This ethic has formed the framework from which we derive implicit positive rewards as a result of the work we do. We gain a sense of self-respect when we demonstrate initiative, industriousness, productivity and self-discipline, all traits valued in the workplace.[5]

If we are chairing the board of a nonprofit organization, raising a quarter of a million dollars for the art museum or getting up three times a week at 5:00 A.M. to oversee the local soup kitchen, we likely are deriving great meaning from these endeavors. They demonstrate our ability and commitment to achieve and complete tasks.[6]

And by being busy, we are protected from the perception that others may have of us as no longer being able to perform. Keeping busy may give definition to our emerging role, which can be clouded at best.[7] It motivates us to continue contributing to society, families, the arts and the nonprofit world. We try to make this world a better place. The key is to find value in our busyness.

A retired executive director in Project Renewment shared her uneasiness when asked, "What are you doing with yourself these days?" "I would mention so many activities that people would gasp at the number of my commitments. But what I was doing had little or no social value. I felt that others perceived me as being shallow and that my life lacked purpose."

The American author Barbara Ehrenreich writes that "the secret of the truly successful . . . is that they learned very early in life how *not* to be busy."[8] This suggests that life is to be savored and not rushed.

When busyness no longer has meaning, it is time to stop, take stock and figure out what is missing in our lives. The board meetings may become tedious, the book clubs may be getting arduous and the gym may become boring.

Maintaining a busy schedule is not the same as being fulfilled. Being busy without meaning implies that quantity is better than quality. Most of us want that quality of life with activities and relationships that replenish our soul and have personal meaning. Being too busy may prevent our continued growth as suggested by the German classical scholar and philosopher Friedrich Nietzsche. "A man [woman] who is very busy seldom changes his [her] opinions."[9]

Questions to ask yourself:
1. How do you feel about unscheduled time?
2. Assuming you will have fifty unscheduled hours of time per week, what will bring you pleasure and satisfaction?
3. How would you define a quality activity?
4. If you want to keep a busy schedule, do you know why?
5. How do you want to balance your time between leisure and activity?

13

MORE THAN THE BLUES

Our greatest glory is not in never falling, but in rising every time we fall.

—Confucius

"Since I retired I don't know what to do with myself," began a social worker. "All I look forward to is going to bed at night. I know I don't want to work—at least for a while. I am still burned out from my job. I thought having free time would be wonderful. Instead, the free time feels like an ocean I have to fill. I don't have any hobbies—I don't play golf or tennis. I work out in a gym when I can get myself there. Lately, I just don't have any energy to do anything. I feel ashamed of how I am feeling and I don't want anyone to know what I am going through. I have always been successful. I pretend to be okay when I am not, but it is getting harder for me to conceal my feelings."

The hopelessness, shame and despair of this retired executive are typical symptoms of depression. They are often accompanied by difficulty sleeping, losing or gaining weight, withdrawing from social activities, having low self-esteem and not being able to focus or make decisions. This is more than feeling "blue."

Feeling sad and anxious as a reaction to change is normal, particularly when we stop working. We miss many aspects of our work life. We may also get frustrated by the time it takes to find stimulating and interesting new activities. Feeling down is normal. However, if symptoms continue it is a signal to get help.

Depression is an emotional as well as a physical illness that should be taken seriously. The good news is that depression is treatable. The bad news is that most people do not seek treatment.[1] Sometimes it is because of a lack of awareness. Other times it is because the person is just too depressed to ask for help, or more likely the individual is ashamed to acknowledge the illness.

In the United States almost 10 percent or about nineteen million people in the U.S. experience depression each year.[2] By 2020, it is projected that depression will be the second leading cause of disability; heart disease will be first.[3] Women are two to three times more likely than men to become depressed[4] and it affects one in four women and one in ten men at some time in their lives.[5]

The National Institute of Mental Health considers depression among those sixty-five and older to be a major public health problem. It affects six to seven million older adults, most of them women, and just 10 percent get treated.[6] Of the nearly thirty-five million people over sixty-five, about two million have a depressive illness and another five million have depressive symptoms that fall short of meeting the diagnostic criteria.[7]

There is no single cause of depression. Sometimes it runs in families. Other times people suffer with no family history. A stressful life change can be a contributing factor, and retirement is one of those traumatic changes, particularly if it means adjusting to a role that, at least initially, feels less than satisfying.

Retirement can be a letdown. Some Project Renewment women said they felt more successful in their careers than they did in their roles as homemakers. For them, work was more fun and rewarding than doing household chores. Women acknowledged these sentiments while at the same time recognizing the love and affection they felt for their children, grandchildren and spouses. But the fact remains— cleaning and cooking simply may not compete with the highs of a job that has intellectual stimulation, problem solving, teamwork, validation, recognition and so much more.

Little is known about the relationship of retirement and depression specifically for career women. Studies conducted in the 1970s found that, in general, when compared to men, women had more negative attitudes toward retirement, felt that retirement was more disruptive to their lives and experienced greater loneliness and depression.[8] These findings may reflect women's disadvantaged positions.[9] A more recent study found that women enter retirement with higher initial levels of depression and lower morale, personal control and perceived inadequacy of their income.[10] We are uncertain whether or not such findings apply to career women.

Although knowledge about retirement is important, it is no guarantee in avoiding depression. One of the women in the group reported that her career as a psychotherapist did not prevent her from becoming depressed herself. "I soon learned that being an expert did not prevent my own struggle. I found that talking to another therapist was helpful. The understanding of my family and friends helped the most."

One major contributor to depression among older persons has nothing to do with work; it has to do with culture. We live in a society where youth is valued over age. The media, entertainment, advertising and fashion industries are prime examples. Aging in a youth culture can create and affirm feelings of worthlessness and of being without a role to play. Perhaps it is no coincidence that the United States has one of the highest estimated rates of depression of almost any country in the world.[10]

Untreated depression in older adults is more likely to lead to suicide than in any other age group. In 2000, those sixty-five and older accounted for almost 13 percent of the population and over 18 percent of all suicide deaths.[12]

Sometimes there are ways to prevent depression in retirement. It helps if we know ourselves and our priorities, and we have a support network of friends, family and colleagues. Ideally, it is healthy to begin defining our roles and identity—before we retire. Acknowledging the illness, knowing it is treatable plus using everything in our personal and professional portfolio that has made us successful in our careers, will help us get through—and over—depression. Simply recognizing and knowing we are depressed is the first step in recovery.

Depression, although unwanted, does serve as an opportunity for growth. We learn what we need to do to stay healthy. "I discovered that regular exercise and a healthy diet is as important to my mental health as it is to my physical health." We have a slight advantage over men; we are more likely to seek help and have a natural tendency to reach out to other women—signs of both health and healing.

The National Institute on Aging indicates that an individual should see a doctor if he or she has several of the following symptoms for more than two weeks:[13]

- a feeling of emptiness, sadness and anxiety;
- feeling tired with no energy;
- losing interest or pleasure in everyday activities, including sex;
- having difficulty sleeping, getting to sleep and waking up early or sleeping too much;
- eating more than usual;
- crying often;
- aches and pains that don't disappear even with treatment;

- difficulty focusing, recalling or making decisions;
- feeling hopeless, worthless and helpless;
- being irritable; and
- having thoughts of suicide or death, or attempting suicide.

Pulitzer Prize–winning author William Styron, wrote about his own severe depression, "whoever has been restored to health has almost always been restored to the capacity for serenity and joy, and this may be indemnity enough for having endured the despair beyond despair."[14]

Questions to ask yourself:

1. Do you experience symptoms of depression? If yes, how long do these symptoms last?
2. Who can you turn to when you are feeling "blue" or depressed?
3. What kinds of things depress you?
4. What makes you feel better when you are depressed?
5. Who are the people that make up your support system?

14

BACK TO THE KITCHEN

What my mother believed about cooking is that if you worked hard and prospered, someone else would do it for you.

—Nora Ephron

"I am a CPA who just retired from a large accounting firm. My husband thinks I am going to return to the kitchen and bake pecan pies. I never liked to bake and I hate pecans." Women in Project Renewment understood her feelings.

Some believe that women who spent their time as full-time homemakers and mothers before the Betty Friedan era will be satisfied

71

returning to those roles in retirement. This is legend. In the late 1950s and early 1960s, most of us were domestic engineers of our households and families. We cooked, baked, shopped, entertained, planned and enabled members of our family to become successful and happy. We established our careers as an important "add-on" to our domestic roles. As time passed, we wanted more and achieved it. Now, if full-time domestic roles were inadequate for us thirty to forty years ago, it is unlikely that at our life stage, the exclusive housewife role will be the center of our lives and our primary source for meaning.

A sixty-two-year-old speech pathologist talked about her experience. "My first experience of having a deep sense of myself as a competent, capable and successful woman came through my work. I married when young and had two children by the time I was twenty-five. While I loved my children, I quickly learned that being a stay-at-home mom was not for me. Once I was working my husband and I shared household responsibilities. We ate out a lot or brought food in. When I retire, I don't want to go back to our old pattern where everything at home becomes my domain. I am sure that is going to surprise and disappoint my husband."

Career women have not completely left the kitchen. Some choose to be there. The "cook and bottle washer" role often is part of retirement, but may not be the only one. Some find cooking, particularly gourmet cooking, more enjoyable now than at any other time in life. "The children were picky," said a college dean. "Now cooking is fun; I can be more creative and my husband joins me."

Other women chimed in with their feelings. "I have found cooking a challenge and thrilling at this time in my life. I am attempting to lower my cholesterol by diet, not drugs. It can be done. My cholesterol went down from 240 to 201 in just a few months."

"Cooking is more than just meal preparation. It relates to my health, and I want this time to be the healthiest in my life. I have changed my lifestyle to make that happen. And how I cook is part of that change."

Many of our mothers were homemakers, queens of the kitchen and often highly dependent on their husbands. "My mother took care of all the domestic chores and also wanted to be taken care of. She couldn't write a check and was proud of it. Her spending money came from my father, who gave her a weekly allowance."

Despite the dependent role, we have warm memories of our mothers in the kitchen. The college dean continued, "As a young child I lived with my parents behind a grocery store. We were crowded into three small rooms, and I vividly remember the comfort I felt sitting with my mother around our stove. The kitchen was where our family came together. It was filled with sweet aromas and my mother's love."

However we may view our kitchen roles, we may have definite ideas about how much time we want to give to managing our home. The CPA continued to say, "Taking care of a household is a lonely experience. I need to get out of my house and mingle with people in order to stay sane. Even though I will have less money when I retire, I will not give up my once-a-week household help."

"Going back to the kitchen" is a metaphor that touches our self-concept, values, health, relationships and roles. The "kitchen" used to define the role of women and their femininity. In many cases, that role was perceived as subservient. Careers added new dimensions to women's identities that need not be given up in retirement.

A market researcher commented, "I don't want to become boring. I need to do things that give me something to talk about. When I was first married, I used to stand in a corner at parties, because I was too shy and insecure to circulate and talk to other people. As soon as I went back to work after my children started school, I felt a surge of self-confidence. I don't want to lose that feeling."

The concerns of these women are well-founded. Their identity has evolved around their success on the job. They are looking for a new model of life as retirees. While husbands may envision their wives resuming old roles, many women will define new ones.

In the 1950s, the slogan "a woman's place is in the home" was well accepted. The updated version, *A Woman's Place Is in the House: Campaigning for Congress in the Feminist Era*, is the title of a book by Barbara Burrell on women running for politics.[1] Returning home after a full-time and rewarding career can be a time of creativity, relaxation and, yes, even cooking. But the domestic return may not be for everyone. Shirley Conran, columnist, editor and author of *Superwoman*, writes, "Life is too short to stuff a mushroom."[2]

Questions to ask yourself:

1. What aspects of your pre-career life did you enjoy?
2. What does the "kitchen role" mean to you?
3. What is the role of your spouse or partner in household tasks and responsibilities? Are they different from when you were working?
4. How can you renegotiate household responsibilities with your spouse or partner when you retire?
5. What physical and/or emotional changes affect your ability to do household chores?

15

GOING IT ALONE

Independence is happiness.

—SUSAN B. ANTHONY

A retired special-education teacher opened a group discussion by saying, "When I was growing up, single women were looked upon as pitiful widows, divorcees or 'old maids.' I was told that there was nothing worse for a woman than to live alone. I believed that until I was divorced, which is the time I learned about freedom—the most positive aspect of being single."

A gerontologist said, "To be single as a widow is not fun, particularly if you had a great marriage. There are those moments, even after years

75

of living alone, that just pierce your soul. I recall coming home after a Saturday morning Sabbath service filled with spirit, music, life and community. Even though I knew better, I was surprised when I opened the front door of my home and walked into the stillness of a well-furnished living room that felt hollow and barren. The contrast was profound and painful."

Single people make up one of the fastest-growing segments of the United States population.[1] Much of that growth is among older adults. In 2004, 43 percent of women sixty-five and older were single because they lost their spouses; among men sixty-five and older, it was 14 percent.[2] Four percent of older single women have never married.[3] Between these two groups, almost half of women sixty-five and over are single, and this does not include those who are divorced.

As a group, widows are quite young; their average age is fifty-six years. Widowed women outnumber widowed men almost three to one.[4] Just scan the Florida landscape and observe what happens when a man becomes available. Dinner invitations, little gifts, phone calls and "the casserole ladies" abound. With increased longevity, particularly for women, it is predicted that we are likely to spend more of our adult years single than married.

Our single Project Renewment women discussed a vision of their future.

- "I would like to keep my independence while still sharing my life with a man."
- "I don't want to deal with the needs, wants, routine or preferences of another human being on a daily basis. And I don't want to be disturbed by anyone else's snoring."
- "I would be happy with a male companion who lived in his own place."
- "I want to be the sole decision-maker for my life. I don't want to consult with anyone else about what I want to buy or where I want to go."

- "I would consider marriage again, if it were the right man."
- "I want to be able to travel whenever I want to, wherever I want to go. Once there, I only want to do the things I feel like doing."
- "I want my personal time and my personal space."
- "I do not want to take care of a man who is sick and infirm. I have watched my friends do this and that's not for me."
- "I like men and would welcome a relationship."

The themes of freedom, independence and companionship were central to the discussions.

Living alone has both an up and a down side. From a positive perspective living alone allows us more time to focus on ourselves. There is less grocery shopping, fewer meals to prepare, less scheduling and domestic work. For some of us this alone time is a relief. One woman who retired a year after her divorce believed she never would have been as engaged and creative in retirement if she had stayed married.

"Each time I ditched my husbands, I blossomed. When I knew I was going to retire, I did a lot of networking to learn about what others did in their retirement. I took risks and tried new things that sometimes didn't work for me. I now find that the untapped creative part of me is flourishing and I continue to explore. If I were still married, I would have felt that I had to leave more time to spend with my husband."

For others, becoming a single woman is a constant reminder of a loss. It means cooking for one or not at all, missing the company and companionship and having no one with whom to share a life.

Regardless of marital status, women share a common fear of being alone in old age. Married women know they have a good chance of outliving their husbands and at some time are likely to be alone. They fear facing declining health or physical limitations without a caring spouse or partner.

One of the most difficult questions we ask ourselves as single women is "Who will be there for me?" We may feel isolated without our work colleagues and the social networks that are, or were, part of our careers. And being the sole financial provider is unnerving. The other lurking and ever-present worry is "Will I have enough money to see me into old age?"

The special-education teacher continued by saying, "I miss the companionship and knowing that there is someone who really gives a darn about what happens to me. But at this time of my life I don't want to spend an evening with a man who is boring. And I don't want to give energy to singles events. The ideal would be to have a companion in my life, but not on a full-time basis."

A social worker commented, "I have made new friends with single women. We are on the same page. I don't have to explain myself to them. I still see a few of my married friends. What I don't like is hearing a woman friend say to me that she will go to see a movie with me because her husband doesn't want to see it. I think to myself, 'Am I chopped liver?'"

An attorney attested to her financial independence: "I have no need for anyone to provide for me. I meet men who cannot be alone and want constant companionship. They want someone to cook for them and do their laundry. It's more difficult to find the right companion later in life so I prefer to spend time alone or with my women friends."

Whether alone because of death or divorce, single women face the future as women who need to adapt to a new status. Once past the managing-change stage of adjustment, we have the opportunity to create a midlife adolescence for ourselves, a time to rediscover and develop parts of ourselves that can blossom and even explode.

The wisdom and experience acquired during our lifetime is an asset. We are positioned to get to know ourselves better by focusing on what we believe are the most enriching parts of life. The next step is to determine what we need to do to experience them.

Questions to ask yourself:

1. How do you envision your life in retirement?
2. What are your concerns?
3. What steps can you take to ensure you have the support you need?
4. Whose company do you most enjoy?
5. How can you ensure that you have enough contact with people?

16

PASSION: IT'S MORE THAN A FRUIT

Chase your passion, not your pension.

—Dennis Waitley

Passion is defined as any "powerful or compelling feeling—grief, joy, love, anger, hate, fear"[1] and has a personal meaning for many Renewment women. Our quest to continue living exciting, compelling lives is called into question when we think about retirement. "Will I ever find passion in my retirement years? I don't know. My life is good as it is. But I wonder if I can still experience that excitement I had when I was president of a dynamic start-up company?" The burning question for those looking to the next chapter of life is whether or not we will be passionate about what we do.

For many of us, stimulating work has driven (or continues to drive) our enthusiasm and commitment. Our energies were ignited by being creative, collaborating in new ways and producing stellar products or services. We felt strongly about being first and/or best.

"I feel passionate when I am stimulated, engrossed and care about something. It is what I think about at night and look forward to in the morning. It's what makes me feel alive," says a theatrical producer.

Throughout our lifetime passion has been a source of intense energy;[2] fuel that motivated us to master tasks, achieve goals and share ourselves with others. It is the impetus for creativity and experiencing a sense of wholeness, integrity and peace.[3] Passion is evident in our play, in our search for meaning and in our contributions to a legacy. Each of us has the capacity to experience these passion-driven purposes at different life stages and in various combinations.

Passion might feel like too strong a word and a concept that takes us beyond our comfort zone. Rather, we may "enjoy," "appreciate" and "like" a variety of endeavors such as photography, acting, travel or being a grandparent. We may not feel passionate about them. For some of us, words and phrases such as love of work, commitment, joy and being deeply engaged more accurately describe our feelings.

Passion-driven purpose changes over time. We are now in the right place to pursue endeavors that may have been impossible during our career years. And as our priorities change, the time has come to let go of judgments about what intensely absorbs us.

One executive found to her surprise that after years in the corporate world she realized she was a homebody. She became involved in local volunteering, piano lessons and gardening. "I never knew that I would feel passionate about the plants on my patio."

Another woman working in the nonprofit world loved sharing ideas with her staff and board of directors. She wanted to re-create a similar connection in the retirement phase of her life. Although she never considered herself a "groupie," she started a series of women's discussion groups.

Passion that stirs our souls can be consuming to the point of losing ourselves. One woman in Project Renewment told us that she forgot to come home for Thanksgiving dinner because she and her colleague were immersed in debugging a new charge-card system. Her guests waited patiently until dinner was finally served by her less than happy husband.

Leaving one's passion is not easy. Between the last days of employment and the beginning of retirement, we may feel we are living in a vacuum.[4] This gray period of transition can be used as a time of exploration, a gift of time for an inner dialogue that may lead to new and meaningful aspects of our lives.

A management consultant commented, "For the first time of my life I have time to support friends who are having health problems. I feel passionate about spending time with them. I consider the available time a blessing."

Feeling passionate about everything and anything has become a hot button and social expectation. Passion may not be for everyone — all of the time. One of our women is a successful marketing consultant working from her home for the past thirty years. She started the company when women realized they could have a career and still be at home with their children. Initially, she was vigorously passionate about her work, the company and its potential. She continues to enjoy her work, but does not have the same energized feeling she had thirty years ago. "It is difficult to sustain passion, doing the same thing year after year. However, new things have drawn me in and yes, I feel passionate about them. Skiing and travel are among them."

If we find we are not deeply engaged in our activities, or have little sense of joy in our lives, it's time to ask, "Is something seriously wrong?"

When our careers have supplied the fuel, keeping the inner fire alive can be difficult. Nathaniel Branden, father of the self-esteem movement and author of several books on the subject,[5] suggests there is a way out. To maintain enthusiasm we need to "appreciate the positives in our lives and [have] a commitment to action."[6] He suggests that we ask ourselves two questions: "What is good in life?" and "What needs to be done?"[7] The first affirms the positive; the second reminds us that we are responsible for our own fulfillment and happiness.[8]

Having a zest for life and all that it affords us has an appeal to career women who love(d) their work. Without becoming compulsive, neurotic or overly stressed, we are warned by humanitarian Dr. Albert Schweitzer to be on alert for slippage:

"'There exists a sleeping sickness of the soul. . . . As soon as you notice the slightest sign of indifference, the moment you become aware of the loss of a certain seriousness, of longing, of enthusiasm and zest, take it as a warning. You should realize your soul suffers if you live superficially."[9]

Questions to ask yourself:

1. How do you define passion?
2. Was/is passion part of your work?
3. Did the thing you felt passionate about change over time?
4. Is passion part of your retirement agenda? If yes, how do you envision it?
5. Where do you find passion outside of your work?

17

YOU CAN ALWAYS VOLUNTEER

If you want to lift yourself up, lift up someone else.

—Booker T. Washington

"You can always volunteer." These are the first words many of us hear from well-meaning friends and relatives upon retirement. With a possibility of thirty years available after our primary careers, this is an opportune time to give back and make a contribution to society. Many do and some don't.

Most of us have volunteered throughout our work life, have thoroughly enjoyed it and now would like to take a break. One woman who served on several boards said, "I don't want to sit on any more boards and prefer not to do any more fund-raising or 'friend-raising.' And I don't want to give away my services since I worked so hard to gain my skills and expertise." Several women didn't want to do "busy work" while others didn't want to be supervised by an inexperienced person. Some just wanted to be free for a period of time from commitments. "I have just been liberated and don't want to have any demands on my time."

Project Renewment women also approached volunteering with gusto. "In a volunteer position, you can experiment and explore new interests without fear; the risks are low." "You get a lot of mental stimulation and have more control over your time with greater flexibility." "I like settings where volunteers are very much appreciated; it's a good feeling." One woman taught children from Third World countries to take photos; another launched a book group and other women committed themselves to the arts as docents and board members.

The challenge is to find the right position. "If you want (volunteering) to be a significant part of your life, then it's likely going to take some work to figure out the right fit," says John Gomperts, CEO of Experience Corps, a nonprofit organization based in Washington, D.C., that solves social problems such as literacy by engaging volunteers who are over fifty-five years old.[1] He adds that "Sometimes you take a very bumpy road to a very beautiful place."[2] That road can begin with an interview conducted by someone less savvy than the potential volunteer who is interviewed.

Kelly Greene, journalist for the *Wall Street Journal*, asked the advice of retirement consultants, nonprofit executives and retirees on ways to avoid the volunteer trap defined as devoting time and energy to a dead-end position.[3] Here is their advice:

- "Identify what inspires you." This is the first step. It sounds easy but few of us have taken the time to identify a cause or mission that motivates us, that moves our soul.
- "Don't be afraid to start at the bottom." If our work has been close to the top, it's hard to start at the bottom. When volunteer-

ing, consider a lower-level position, letting those around you know you have different or higher aspirations and are willing to learn the ropes.

- "Know when to make a change." Determine if you want to try something new or volunteer in a way that uses proven skills and expertise.
- "Protect your time." We need to determine how much time we want to contribute to a volunteer endeavor. Our time should not be wasted or misused. It is as important as it was pre-retirement. It's called a life.
- "Look for good training." Some groups offer this; others do not. Training and educational opportunities can provide stimulation, new knowledge and "know-how," and opportunities to meet others.
- "Keep [very] flexible." Organizations shift and change as do their leadership, missions and budgets. We may be convinced that the position is perfect for us and then funding runs out, the staff changes and the activities are reduced. All of this may affect our eagerness and high expectations.

Finding the right volunteer role can be as difficult as finding the right job. When pursuing a volunteer position, ask the individual who is interviewing you the following questions:

1. What is the mission of the organization?
2. Can you tell me about its history?
3. What is your source of funding?
4. Can I see your financial statement?
5. Who is on your board of directors?
6. Given my background, what position(s) would you recommend?
7. What do you consider the organization's strengths and weaknesses?
8. How many volunteers do you have?
9. Is there an orientation period?
10. How do you recognize the achievements of your volunteers?

11. What are the time and schedule commitments?
12. Will there be someone to cover for me if I am not available?

Another suggestion is to create our own position if an interesting role is not available. We may create one that will help the organization fulfill its mission and one that speaks to our strengths.

Volunteering has benefits beyond personal fulfillment. A study of 128 volunteers, 60 to 86 years old who worked with children in Baltimore schools, were compared to a control group. The volunteers were in better health, burned more calories, watched less TV and reported having more people in their lives than those who did not volunteer.[4]

Although little research has been conducted specifically on career women and volunteering, one study found that career women tend to pursue volunteer activities that use their proven expertise from their previous work.[5] A retired accountant may serve as the treasurer of a nonprofit board, or an architect may serve on the building committee of a school, church or synagogue. Professional women tended to blend their careers into retirement pursuits as volunteers. That was not the case for noncareer women, who were inclined to volunteer for tasks and activities different from their work roles.[6]

As we look to our future, we might consider stepping out of our comfort zone to try something novel. The risks are low, and the potential for growth, new experiences and contributing to society in a new way can be rewarding and fun.

Questions to ask yourself:

1. Do you want to volunteer in ways similar to your work experience?
2. Do you want single or multiple volunteer positions?
3. Do you ultimately want a leadership or "follower-ship" role?
4. What are you looking for in a volunteer experience? To make a difference, a new way to structure your time, make use of your current skills, establish new social relationships or find a new challenge?
5. How will you pursue a volunteer opportunity?

18

WHAT DO I WEAR WHEN I AM NOT IN A BUSINESS SUIT?

When in doubt, wear red.

— BILL BLASS

We've come a long way. In the 1970s, our fashion goal was to blend in with the male work world. We underplayed our feminine side with conservative suits. Under our tailored jacket with a proper pin in our lapel, we wore a long-sleeved blouse with a silk scarf tied under our neck—a variation of a bow tie. We wanted to look attractive and make the best fashion decisions. Some of us got our "colors done," which involved determining our color palette based on our skin and hair color. The colors were organized according to the seasons of the year. Winter meant we looked good in cool colors such as purple, white and black; fall colors such as gold, brown and orange were warm.

In the 1980s and 1990s we branched out of the fashion box, but not without frustration. Retailers seemed to ignore the millions of Boomer women and those slightly older who dressed for work. Finding conservative clothes became a challenge. Skirts were above the knee and blouses were fluffy with ruffles. Following then first lady Hillary Clinton, who frequently appeared in pants suits, trousers and jackets became the dress of the day.

Then came retirement. A fifty-eight-year-old corporate administrator talked about her experience. "Going into my closet was a shock. It was my first week of retirement. My wardrobe consisted of nothing but suits and the pair of jeans I wore on the weekend. The first time I went out to lunch with friends after I retired, I had nothing to wear. I looked around at the nonworking women and realized I needed a more casual wardrobe. That concerned me as my budget for new clothing was limited without a regular paycheck. Once out shopping, I felt even more alienated. The store windows and the merchandise inside were not geared for the fifty-plus woman. I couldn't find anything I even wanted to try on. The hip-hugging, layered clothing did not make sense with my mature body. I immediately realized that I was behind the times and definitely not hip. I wanted to put together a new look for myself, but I didn't want to look matronly. I have a decent enough figure and wanted to show it off. Besides, I still feel young."

Accommodating new purchases meant it was time to clean out the closet. The task serves many purposes. In addition to making room in our closet, it gives us a sense of immediate accomplishment, order and even predictability. We begin by deciding what we can salvage in our wardrobe. A great old jacket may look terrific with a pair of jeans. After some creative juggling, we decide what has to go and then are faced with the next decision—what to do with the discarded business suits, skirts, pants and jackets, and those beautiful silk blouses?

A stockbroker found a way to deal with the discards. "After not wearing most of my suits I knew I had to put them to good use before the moths did. I discovered an organization that assists homeless women returning to the workforce. They were in need of business attire and I found it rewarding to know clothes that had just been hanging in my closet would be put to good use."

For some, the challenge of "what to wear" is more liberating than frustrating.

A retired human resource specialist achieved a new sense of freedom. "I haven't worn a pair of panty hose or high-heeled shoes since I retired. I go around in sweats, blue jeans, tennis shoes and a very casual outfit for dressier occasions. Retiring my suits and accessories is one of the best parts of retirement. I love my freedom to wear whatever I want."

"I never wear panty hose," commented a retired accountant. "I cannot believe I did that every day in my corporate life. It's cathartic just being rid of them."

Many of us were schooled on how to dress for success. The American Management Association offered courses, books were written and read, and corporate, university and nonprofit environments had expectations about what was considered proper attire. Many still do. Few of us wanted to buck the system, so we complied. We were used to the conformity.

As our preferences have changed, slowly, very slowly the choices of available clothing have changed. Retailers have discovered what they believe is a new market—the older consumer, otherwise known as the mature market. Loosely identified, this population includes both men and women, fifty years and older, who have approximately $2 trillion of spending power.

This market is not new. We have been around for years. What has pushed the apparel industry are the Boomers who are aging both in and out of the workplace. Their power comes from their numbers, seventy-eight million men and women comprising the largest cohort in history. In addition to the forty million women in the Boomer generation, there are an additional thirty-two million who are older.[1]

"Companies have set their sights on the graying crowd quite simply because they're seeing green."[2] Chico's, the women's apparel store, was one of the first to tap this market.[3] They use a simple dress-size system and offer clothing that is loose-fitting and made from natural fabrics and they have a helpful staff to create wardrobes. Designer Sigrid Olsen caters to women thirty-five to fifty-five. The classically designed clothing of Talbots and Ann Taylor also appeals to midlife women.

There are others. Guess introduced the Marciano chain for the slightly older sophisticated consumer who wants fancy jeans and glittering evening dresses.[4] Levi's introduced relaxed jeans, which accommodate the changing physical dimensions of Boomers.

A Clinique advertisement says it well: "Beauty isn't about looking young, but looking good." This should serve as a reminder to clothing designers. Is it possible to look good and still be comfortable? Consider the approach taken by the late comedian Gilda Radner: "I base my fashion taste on what doesn't itch."[5]

Questions to ask yourself:

1. When is the last time you cleaned your clothing closet?
2. If you clean out the clutter in your closet, how would you sort your clothes?
3. What clothing can you still use? Which garments have meaning to you?
4. What charitable organization could use your clothing?
5. What friend would you take shopping with you to get that new look?

19

GRANDCHILDREN: FINDING THE BALANCE

When a child is born, so are grandmothers.

— Judith Levy

"Oh my God, I am so tired. I've been taking care of my three-year-old granddaughter while my daughter is taking care of her new-born son. I feel as if I have just given birth. I finally told my daughter that I had to take the afternoon off. I do feel guilty."

Energy is not something we thought about in our middle years. We cared for our children, hosted dinner parties, drove car pools, pursued our careers and served as family nurse, psychologist, planner, educator and decorator. We worked, were good mothers, supportive wives and played a role in the community. Operating in overdrive, we managed to get everything done and still smile, at least most of the time.

When we realize there is a discrepancy between what we want to do and what we are able to do, we may have a problem. For highly effective women, our expectations may be unrealistic and modifying our behavior can be difficult.

A physical therapist had a vision of what it would be like as a grandparent. "I expected to prepare meals for the new parents while caring for my newborn grandchild, my husband and my mother. I quickly came face-to-face with the fact that I was sixty-five, not thirty-five years old."

Some things have changed. We are a generation of women living longer and healthier lives than at any time in U.S. history. At the same time, many of us have noticed we have less energy than we had in our mothering years and recovery time from overexertion takes longer. Knowing these changes are part of the normal aging process has not made adapting easier.

We also are a new generation of women who have established a life and identity separate from the family. Many of us are still finding our way in the transition from work to retirement. During this change, family is likely our keystone, but may be only one of several important elements in our lives.

A therapist commented that since she retired her children tell her they want her to be more involved with their family. "They would like me to designate one day a week to care for my grandchildren. They seem to think I have morphed into a Donna Reed, Betty Crocker grandmother. The reality is that my schedule changes from week to week and I don't want to be that programmed. I am still struggling with my own transition. It's hard to say 'no' because I love them and my grandchildren. I just want more flexibility in the time we spend together."

Becoming a grandparent is an experience that provides many of us with unending fulfillment, pleasure and fun. We have the opportunity to make up for the time we missed with our own children as we were juggling child rearing with a demanding career. The Renewment life stage is a time to renew and focus on family.

If we worked for a large company, the limits were established for us. Time off was dictated by company policies on dependent care, maternity leave, sick time and vacation days. Now we have to establish our own days off and the corresponding boundaries.

When our children cannot afford a nanny or a babysitter, the grandmother often is asked to substitute. If we are newly retired, we may be eager to spend as much time as possible with our grandchildren. When we get those desperate phone calls for help, we are there. Regardless of what we are doing, we find it painful to decline the request, even if we are exhausted. Part of us may still want to be "superheroes"—doing it all once again. And if we decline to babysit our grandchildren, it is easy to feel guilty and selfish because we are tending to our own needs rather than those of our children and grandchildren. Babysitting and a visit are different. Few of us would say "no" to a grandchild who says, "Grandma, I miss you. Please come to my house." We are there.

"When I became a grandparent it was the most amazing experience of my life," noted a teacher. "I got the joy of being with my grandchildren without the burden of full-time responsibility. When I am with them they get my full attention. This is a far cry from the stress I see in my children, who are stretched to the limit. I realize how much they miss and how much I missed when they were growing up. It makes me wonder about some of the decisions I made as a young mother."

Not everyone has had the idealized grandparent role. An increasing number of grandparents are raising grandchildren at a time when they thought they were free of family responsibilities. Time with Grandma can become an issue when grandchildren live far away or are over-booked.

A business consultant was heartbroken over the amount of time she had with her granddaughter. "Her mother keeps her scheduled and usually unavailable for planned or spontaneous activities with me. My granddaughter goes from school to extracurricular activities during the week. On the weekends she is scheduled with birthday parties and playdates with friends. Time with Grandma is not a priority." E-mail has been a boon to staying in touch, but it never can replace the hugs, kisses and just being there.

"I used to think that my grandfather's saying 'Thank you for coming and thank you for going' was an uncaring statement to his grandchildren," said one of our women. "His words ring true for me now. Being a grandmother is the most enthralling and most exhausting job I have ever had. I am thrilled I can enjoy my grandchildren, spoil them and then send them home."

If we wonder why we care so deeply for our grandchildren, it all began a million years ago in the plains of Africa. A mother gave birth to a hominid child after a long and exhausting labor. She barely had enough energy to nurse her baby and not enough energy to feed or care for her older child.[1] Geriatrician Dr. William H. Thomas writes, "A miracle occurred."[2] The maternal grandmother intentionally shared her food with her grandchild. At that moment, a new pattern of support began that carried over to other families. Thomas writes that humans are the only species that have grandparents deliberately helping to raise grandchildren. He calls this grandparent support a "defining characteristic" of humans.[3]

President Jimmy Carter recognized the importance of grandparents when in 1978 he established Grandparents' Day, celebrated on the Sunday after Labor Day.[4] While it is not a day that receives the attention of Mother's or Father's Day, it is a national acknowledgment to honor grandparents' contributions.

Given the opportunity, the relationship between grandparents and grandchildren is the most extraordinary win-win situation. Our grandchildren have our undivided love, attention and caring. In turn, our lives are enriched in ways that go beyond careers and success. In time, grandchildren may help identify and clarify our priorities. We know that the joy they bring to our lives is fleeting and can never be duplicated.

Questions to ask yourself:

1. What kind of relationship would you like to have with your grandchildren? How can you create it?
2. How much time do you want to spend with your grandchildren?
3. How does your relationship with your children influence your relationship with your grandchildren?
4. How have the changes in your life affected your relationship with your grandchildren?
5. What do you want your grandchildren to remember about you?

20

THE QUEEN OF MULTITASKING
IS TAKING A BREAK

*I'm always multitasking. Eating, on the phone,
interview(ing), everything all at once.*

—HEIDI KLUM

The time has come to remove the apple cores and banana peels
from our car, the lunches we ate when we didn't have time to eat a real
lunch. It is time to stop putting on makeup in the rearview mirror and
returning phone calls from the freeway.

Women are the queens of multitasking. Since the hunting and

gathering era, they multitasked as they picked berries, nursed an infant, stirred a pot and watched a little one.[1] The word "multitasking" was introduced around 1966 by the computer industry. It meant the computer had sufficient memory to do more than one thing at a time.[2]

Multitasking for women was an imperative in raising young children, with or without a career. The following scenario from the 1970s may slightly resemble the hunting and gathering era and seem familiar. "I remember holding my six-month-old baby on my hip while stirring a pot on the stove, answering the phone and watching my other little one who wasn't on my hip. Then it was time to set the table for ten dinner guests, pick up the last-minute toys in the entryway so guests would not trip (still with that baby on my hip) and, of course, quickly dressing, brushing my hair and if I was lucky, putting on lipstick that actually landed on my lips. That was multitasking." Mothers did not have the luxury to accomplish their tasks one at a time. If they did, the groceries would still be in the bag, one child would be hungry and the other would still be on the toilet.

Researchers have found that men and women are equally productive in multitasking with no significant difference between them.[3] Other researchers, using results from rat experiments, discovered that multitasking females were more accurate and efficient in tasks performed at the same time.[4] We do need to be cautious in applying results from rat studies to humans.

Yet others have documented a biological difference that may give women the edge. MRIs indicate women have a larger corpus callosum, the area of the brain that handles communication between the two hemispheres and synthesizes information from both sides of the brain.[5] Perhaps our own experience shows which sex, if either, is the better multitasker.

"My husband thinks I am inefficient because I do five things at the same time while he accomplishes one task at a time. He reads the newspaper with his coffee, then makes a few phone calls, followed by going to the quiet of our den for some office work, more reading and then for a walk. I make breakfast, read the headlines, write a grocery list, answer the phone and review my office to-do list all at the same time."

Employers generally value multitasking, believing it possible for a few people to do the work of many without sacrificing quality or cost. It has become the managerial buzzword or mantra to "do more with less." Contrary to the managerial belief system, some research indicates that multitasking has hidden costs and is considered inefficient because of time lost switching between complex tasks.[6]

Perpetual multitasking in our personal life is an indication that it is time to take stock. Something is amiss when we have time to chew our food and get to our next appointment on time, and still find ourselves eating in the car and speeding to our appointments. Effective career women have had to do many things simultaneously to rise through the ranks and reach their level of excellence. But we now have the choice. Rather than keeping up a frenetic style, we can choose to smell the roses, one at a time. We can give ourselves permission to cherish the moment.

One woman told us about setting the table for a holiday dinner. "I was using china that my parents brought over from Germany in 1938. The dinner dishes and coffee set are well over 100 years old. I typically would hurry to get the table set because there was so much to do, or I would do several things in between, such as check e-mail, make a phone call or sort the snail mail. This time I stopped and just gazed at the beautiful porcelain, the gold edges, and thought about the history that these dishes witnessed. It was a moment when I felt I was beginning to move to another level of awareness and control over my thinking and feelings. It was an 'in the moment' experience and quite beautiful."

We are at a life stage where we travel a fine line. No one knows what tomorrow brings. Now is the time to discern, discriminate and relish our time and the ways we fill it. It is time to savor our moments and not permit distractions to diminish quality time. It is hard to slow our thoughts and actions. Practice helps. What a change . . . one thing at a time.

Questions to ask yourself:

1. If you completed a survey of what you do in an hour, what would it include?
2. When are you most likely to multitask?
3. What are your favorite moments to savor?
4. How do you manage and execute your daily tasks and activities?
5. How has multitasking served you in the past? How does it serve you now?

21

DEALING WITH ILLNESS

The more serious the illness, the more important it is for you to fight back, mobilizing all your resources— spiritual, emotional, intellectual, physical.

—Norman Cousins

"I was absolutely shocked when I heard my diagnosis," announced one Project Renewment woman. "I couldn't believe that I could be so healthy and at the same time be so seriously ill. There is nothing that could have prepared me for this interruption in my life."

No one wants to plan for a serious illness or prepare for a life-threatening disease. What we can do is learn from those who are seriously ill.

In our Project Renewment groups we have women who valiantly fought or are fighting illnesses. They are the embodiment of insight and courage and have taught us ways to be supportive and better understand their feelings.

"I like to have people ask for my opinion," she continued. "I am still here. I like to talk about things other than my disease. I know when people are uncomfortable and pussyfoot around my illness. They just don't know what to say. It makes me feel that I am a scary person."

A common response to those who are ill is to give them advice. We may deliver a litany of our own illnesses or those of people we know, hoping other people's challenges and victories will make them feel better. Our cheerleader instinct may encourage the sick to fight against their disease. Although the intentions are good, the message may not always be received in the way intended.

Another woman added, "When people tell me to fight harder it makes me feel that I am not fighting hard enough and that I can control my disease. The one thing I have had to learn is that I do not have control. That has been one of the hardest lessons."

We learned from our women that illness can strengthen relationships. "New people who I never have expected to become my friends have come into my life. I also realized that I need to ask for and accept support, help and nurturing, a rather new role for me."

"When a friend said that she wanted to bring me food, I told her what I really needed were rides to chemotherapy. These times together turned out to be among the most intimate of our long-standing relationship."

Our women being treated for illnesses said their personal adjustments were difficult. "It was a challenge to learn how to rest. I am used to being active and involved. I have to lecture myself that my limited capacity is temporary; at least I hope it is."

Life-threatening illnesses call upon inner resources. Learning what to expect about our illness and recovery may require research and discussion with our physicians and others going through a similar illness. Women in Project Renewment became experts on their conditions. "I told my doctor that we were partners in my health care. I questioned why they do it this way and not the other way. I didn't rely solely on any individual doctor. God bless the Internet. I checked Google and the National Library of Medicine PubMed[1] and many others.[2] I used my time and energy to find out as much as I could about my disease. At times I have come up with information that I shared with my doctor that changed the course of my treatment."

One woman acknowledged that the serious disease of depression was one of the side effects of her life-threatening illness. She shared how she struggled and coped. "I sometimes get overwhelmingly depressed but I try to treat it like I would a headache in order to diminish the pain. I have to believe that I will feel better."[3]

Others turned to religion for solace. "I am in the hands of a greater being. I believe there is a plan for me and I will know that plan at the right time. It comforts me to put myself in God's hands. I am not concerned about the outcome. That is the way it is supposed to be."

A serious illness is life-altering and can change the way a person wants to live. "My illness has been liberating. What used to scare me does no longer. I have nothing to lose. I take risks now that I ordinarily would not take. If I die while I am doing something I enjoy, so be it."

Women commented that their greatest buffer to despair was the support and sensitivity of the people who surrounded them. "They are there for us even when we lose our sense of being valuable or are overwhelmed by our illness."

Renewment group members have stayed connected to the women who are ill. They have phoned, written and visited, bringing warmth, compassion and news of the outside world. These actions are important to women spending most of their time at home or in a facility. Feelings of isolation are pervasive.

Over time, the Renewment women have expanded their relationships with one another beyond retirement issues. They have cared for their "sisters" by providing transportation to physicians and pharmacies, bringing picnic lunches, going for walks, seeing a movie and just being available. They have given warm hugs and reassuring smiles.

These small enduring communities of women are a by-product of Project Renewment and a reservoir of support during our women's highest and lowest moments in life.

Questions to ask yourself:

1. If you or your spouse or partner became seriously ill, what arrangements would have to be made to accommodate the change in health or functioning? What changes would you have to make in your home to accommodate an illness?
2. Do you have all the medical coverage you need? Do you have Medicare and supplemental health insurance?
3. Who would assist you with your business and personal affairs if you became seriously ill?
4. Do you have a health advocate and a living will?
5. Where do you keep all of your important health information? Is it all in one place?

22

PERSONAL PLANNING:
IS IT FOR ME?

*It pays to plan ahead. (After all), it wasn't raining
when Noah built the ark.*

—ANONYMOUS

The importance of planning for financial security in retirement
is a "no-brainer." The earlier, the better. Projecting income and
expenses leads to a plan that creates the best chance to have enough
money for necessities, and hopefully enough to have choices. We may
apply a variety of assumptions and conditions to our financial plan. The

numbers are concrete and can be placed on a spreadsheet for review and modification.

The unquantifiable aspects of retirement typically do not appear on spreadsheets and are often ignored. With about thirty years ahead of us, that's some 175,000 hours of discretionary time. We hope advanced planning for our post-career leads to a good life. Where to live, how to stay healthy and fit, figuring out what to do, the needs of our aging parents and end-of-life issues are all part of the retirement experience. We may ignore these aspects of later life or think about them as priorities that require a plan.

For some, planning is perceived as restrictive. One woman believes, "Too much planning means we may miss the moment. It can get in our way, locking us in mentally. A plan is in bronze, making us feel we have to live by it. We lived most of our lives planning. I feel liberated by not having that pressure. We are living in a beautiful time of life when we can change, be ready and open. It's a time of freedom."

An educator has become more self-conscious about setting priorities as she got older. "It may be that planning in later life is really about making sure we are living our lives in a way that enhances rather than inhibits who we are, and in some way contributes to the world we live in."

She continued to say, "The whole question of planning in this stage of my life is related to my perception of time. Although some days I think I'll probably live another thirty years, I am more aware of living in the present or 'mindfulness' as the Buddhists say. Planning now is related to depth and fullness of living, not to extended time."

Planning for lifestyles may be of equal importance to planning for finances. "I review my financial plan every quarter. I also rank a list of priorities that include health, wealth, family, friends, travel, entertainment, spirituality and learning. Along with my financial plan, I check my priority list once a quarter. If there is no alignment, either the priority is wrong, the ranking is wrong or I am not spending my time in ways that are important to me. I couldn't live my life between planning sessions if I didn't know that both my financial and nonfinancial plan were there. This is a conscious process."

Planning is part of the American way. As newlyweds, we planned for accumulating the dollars needed for a down payment for our first home. We planned for our babies and then for their education. We planned, hopefully, for our own economic security in later life.

If we plan for our post-career, our long-term work experience can provide a clue about what is important to us. To identify such values we can ask ourselves the question: "What are the real benefits of working?"

"(We) work for more than money, honey!" write Jeri Sedlar and Rick Miners, authors of *Don't Retire, Rewire*.[1] This was confirmed by the responses of more than ten thousand long-term employees participating in retirement education programs who were asked a similar question, "Why have you worked for your employer all of these years?" They stayed with their employers because they liked their work and its challenges. They valued the company benefits, their coworkers and the opportunities for growth, travel and advancement. They enjoyed social relationships, making a difference, having a sense of purpose and the power and influence that were part of their job. They also liked the money, although salary typically was not identified by long-term employees as one of the top ten reasons for remaining with their employers.[2]

Women in Project Renewment have acted upon the values and responsibilities that motivated them in their careers. A program analyst who loved challenges became an avid hiker; an attorney who enjoyed developing strategies travels with daunting itineraries to Third World countries. The commitment to women and aging has motivated another to devote almost all her time to leading a growing national organization for midlife women. The value of relationships has inspired another one of our women to spend two days a week taking care of her grandchildren.

A social worker commented, "Part of planning is keeping your fingers crossed. I don't know anyone whose plans worked out exactly as they hoped. We need to remind ourselves that life is unpredictable."

"I am not doing any of the things I said I would do in retirement." This woman was retired for one year and found her experience completely different from what she had planned. Plans can always be remodeled and are never permanent. A plan at sixty may not be the one that we want at age sixty-five, seventy or eighty.

If plans are too rigid, we can become stifled or cramped. The "white spaces" in our lives are a gift to reflect on what we want to do. Our personal plan should be flexible enough for us to take advantage of spontaneous moments for new adventures and endeavors. Although we may believe that anything is possible, acknowledging practical limitations such as family responsibilities, health concerns and finances are part of the process.

Taking risks may make or break our plan. If we fail, we know we can always get up and try something else. Risks are diminished when we have some sort of a strategy or sense of priorities, whether they are long or short term.

Many of us approach commitments and obligations as projects. We are facing the big one. In this Renewment phase of life, we are undertaking one of the most important and long-running projects of our lives—life after work. It is ours to shape.

Questions to ask yourself:
1. What are the most significant benefits you experience or experienced from your work?
2. What activities or actions will enable you to derive similar benefits in your post-career life?
3. Can the planning process you used at work apply to your personal planning?
4. What is the one thing you always wanted to do, see or create? How might you accomplish this?
5. What aspects of your life require the most planning?

23

WHAT IF *HE* RETIRES FIRST?

*When a man retires, his wife gets twice the husband
but only half the income.*

—CHI CHI RODRIGUEZ

"'Honey,' he said, 'I was offered a retirement package I cannot refuse and want to accept the offer. When can you leave your job?' I nearly fell over," said this high-powered business woman.

The timing of a couple's retirement can be complex, particularly when husbands are ready to retire and we are not. Women and men have different retirement timetables for good reasons. Women's work histories were often interrupted by staying home to raise children, relocating with husbands as they furthered their careers and returned to school for advanced degrees. Also, many women are a few years younger than their spouses. As a result, women may reach the peak of their careers as husbands are ready to exit theirs.

The husband of a graphic designer retired while she continued to work. "I am surprised he is doing so little to be helpful. I thought he would have dinner started when I came home or do more around the house. His time is still his own as I continue to have two full-time jobs. After forty years of marriage, I was hoping for more."

"My husband retired before me and would like me to do the same. I love my work as an analyst and hope to get a promotion. He has few men friends and is looking forward to my companionship. I think we are headed for trouble."

These women may be reading the tea leaves correctly. Bumps in a marriage are more likely to occur when men retire before their wives.[1] Research studies have found that retired husbands report they are least satisfied when their wives continue working.[2] For men, the most satisfying retirement is when both husband and wife retire at the same time.[3]

As pre-Boomers, we should not be surprised that men often do not like change. In the early years of marriage most men's major commitment was to their work. They typically did not engage in the hands-on raising of the children and household tasks, and rarely drove carpools or took the kids to the pediatrician. The term "stay-at-home dad" had not yet been invented. Men approached changing a diaper as a onetime engineering event. A dirty diaper was almost a 911 call. Doing the laundry? Cleaning the house? Get real! It didn't happen.

That's not the case today for many modern husbands. Daddies drop off children at preschool, sell Girl Scout Cookies at their law offices, give their children baths, sit in pediatricians' offices and help with chores and grocery shopping. Today, men and women tend to divide family responsibilities on a more equal basis. An indication that such a partnership will likely be sustained in later life is the increase of men providing care to aging parents, a role typically assumed by women.

"While both of us were working, my husband shared in doing errands, household chores, gardening and grocery shopping. As soon as I retired he expected me to take care of everything. This left me little time or energy for myself, and that I resented. Since we had always had good communication, we were able to talk and reach a resolution."

Not all couples score high on communication. In retirement planning, relationships and communication are rarely addressed.[4] Yet we know that couples often do not share the same expectations from one another in retirement. Even with this knowledge, the topic of relationships usually is not included in retirement planning programs.[5] And there are reasons. First, there is the accepted belief that if it's not broken, don't fix it. If a thirty-year marriage has been successful while both spouses are working in their established careers, there seems little reason to discuss relationships. Second, how one gets along with a spouse is a private matter and typically is not discussed in a public forum. The ladies' room rather than the meeting room has become the salon for such discussions. Breaks during formal retirement education programs have revealed interesting comments.

A retirement specialist who conducted retirement education programs overheard the conversation of women participants as they applied lipstick. "I am so glad our facilitator covered the subject of relationships in retirement. I cannot discuss the subject with Harry"—or "George"—or "Tom." Upon returning to the meeting room, these same women were silent.

If we are not used to discussing personal relationships, to start such dialogues at age sixty or sixty-five can be difficult. As a generation that did not focus on "talking things through," we may lack the skills and self-confidence. Habits of omission or silence are hard to break.

"My husband was ecstatic when I retired. But it was not for long. I got involved in several nonprofit organizations and took on a number of leadership roles. I was thrilled. He was disappointed that my activities meant that I would have less time for him. One of the hardest things for me is to go off to do my activities and leave him home alone with nothing to do."

Relationships with our mates may take some work. "While we were both working we didn't have time to work on our marriage. I was surprised at how much of a strain we felt once we were home together. We shared an office that he kept in a state of constant turmoil. He didn't want me to move any of his papers. When I was working on some of my own projects I would have to hear his radio or his voice booming on the phone. The first thing we had to do was to convert one of our bedrooms into a separate office. Having our own space saved our marriage."

Ben Franklin suggested we keep our eyes wide open before marriage and half shut afterward.[6] Women of Project Renewment are wide-eyed. We want to share these precious years with our spouses while still having time for ourselves. It's a time to be supportive and encourage respective outside commitments that will enrich our relationships in general. But most of all this is a time to be good to one another.

Questions to ask yourself:

1. How best can you communicate with your spouse or significant other about being retired together?
2. How would your husband's retirement affect you?
3. Would you feel a need to retire at the same time as your husband?
4. When would be your ideal time to retire?
5. What will you tell your husband if he wants you to retire when he does?

24

PLAY

We don't stop playing because we grow old;
we grow old because we stop playing.

—George Bernard Shaw

"I can't remember playing as a child. As the eldest of my siblings, I was engaged in caregiving at a very early age. My parents didn't put any value on play and I grew up thinking the same. I took my work seriously and did not engage in what appeared to be frivolous activities. I now understand what I missed and I need to make up for lost time. I want to learn how to play."

"My parents were immigrants. Work was a way of life [in order] to make it in America. To waste time was almost sinful. Play was an indulgence that was not acknowledged and never rewarded. My parents did not have time for it. It is still difficult to divorce myself from these childhood values. My sister continues to ask me if I had a productive day, rather than asking if I had any fun."

Emerging from structured work environments, we have been playing by company rules, fulfilling employer expectations and receiving the commensurate rewards. Creating and adhering to policies have been part of our careers. We are now in a new phase of life.

"I participated in an art workshop designed for children. The owner invited a dozen adults to just have fun with art. We sat on small chairs and moved from a Play-Doh station to a painting wall to a collage station. I stood in front of the painting wall, facing a large sheet of empty paper. Behind me were pots of tempera paints in brilliant fuchsia, canary yellow, deep purple and azure. I held a large paintbrush with soft bristles between my fingers, unsure of which pot of paint I should dip my brush. The rules were—there are no rules. I was immobile for what seemed like forever, and then I finally dipped into the fuchsia."

Play is any recreational activity that is not work.[1] As conscientious professional women, we may have found that time for play was difficult because of work demands and extensive commitments. During this new life stage, we may need to reprogram ourselves to indulge in play and enjoy it without guilt. As a generation of women who have been socialized to be other-directed, we typically think of those in need and important causes that warrant our energies and talents for the betterment of others. Social responsibility has been part of our training.

Giving ourselves permission to play may take some work. Our grandchildren are one of the best resources for us to learn to play again. Children can play imaginary games all day. To their delight, many of us join them in playing hide-and-seek, good guys–bad guys or pretending to be mommy, daddy or baby. We can play with blissful abandon.

Grandchildren also reacquaint us with belly laughs and silliness. Imaginations can run wild and fantasy is at its best as we play with dollies, attend a tea party or build with LEGOs and Tinkertoys. Such play is like taking a vacation from ourselves. The only rules of the game are to do no harm—to oneself, others or things like Grandma's antique lamp or white sofa.

"As a self-employed person, I have a flexible schedule. When I am stressed with a heavy workload and need a break, I play with my four-year-old grandson. Our latest endeavor was imagining how we could create a flying saucer out of a big box that contained a toy for his brother. Fortunately, we are not at the execution stage of our plan."

The meaning of play varies with the individual. "We need a new definition of play. It's not the fun and games that we played as kids. I believe there are three kinds of play. The first is cultural and intellectual such as a trip to China or Vietnam. The second is super-hedonistic and self-indulgent such as a week at our favorite spa resort. The third is pure play such as snorkeling, skiing or biking. When I am having fun, my soul is rejuvenated and I can more easily move on to what we call productive activities such as work."

Becoming aware of our attitude about play and fun can be stimulated by others. "I recall sitting in a meeting led by a professional group facilitator. As an icebreaker the facilitator asked each one of us to tell the group what we would be doing for fun this coming summer. That was just one year after my husband died. As everyone shared, I started to panic—'What in the world was fun?' I was relieved to tell the group I planned to spend time with my granddaughter. It got worse. That evening I attended a dinner and was seated next to the president of the sponsoring university. We had a nice getting acquainted chat, until he asked me, 'And what do you do for fun?' I decided my inability to discuss this subject was a wake-up call to look at my life."

Scholars and philosophers understood that we reveal our authentic selves when engaged in play. More than two thousand years ago, Plato suggested that "you can discover more about a person in an hour of play than in a year of conversation." And Albert Einstein called play "the highest form of research."[2] The study of play and its role in American culture is the focus of the Strong National Museum of Play in Rochester, New York.[3]

Play is pure, nonjudgmental, creative and fun. Women in Project Renewment gravitated to this kind of experience by forming interest groups, which actually were play groups for adults. The fun activities included hiking, traveling, walking, cycling, knitting, acting and trips to museums, movies, concerts and the theater. One woman hosted evenings of swimming, food and conversation in her garden, providing opportunities for play and laughter. The women found having others to play with was enriching.

Workshops are dedicated to help adults learn to play, providing a safe environment for them to get in touch with their creative selves. "How-to" books are published on the subject. It's hard to imagine self-help resources on the subject of play since it seems so natural; clearly there is a need.

One of the joys and benefits from playing and playfulness is laughter. Not only does laughter makes us feel good, it also boosts the immune system, reduces stress and blood pressure, elevates mood, connects us to others and promotes instant relaxation.[4] We've heard the old expression "laughter is the best medicine." There is some truth to this. Scientists have referred to laughter as an "internal jogging."[5] Research studies find that laughter boosts endorphins, the body's natural painkillers, while suppressing the stress hormone epinephrine.

Adults laugh about fifteen times daily and children about four hundred times a day.[6] Perhaps we have a new assignment in the Renewment phase of life. Have fun, play and laugh a lot!

Questions to ask yourself:

1. What kind of play did you enjoy while growing up?
2. What kind of play is most appealing to you today?
3. What makes you laugh?
4. What makes you feel free?
5. How can you bring play into your life?

25

BUYING THE PLOT

Life is good, without it we'd all be dead.

—Hannah

A seventy-year-old retired educator spoke about her family experience. "My father was an immigrant and a consummate planner. Not only did he purchase plots for himself and my mother, he identified which police in the community would accompany the hearse and the best route to the cemetery. What he couldn't control were the remarks of the presiding clergy. The minister who led the memorial service disliked my father and adored my deceased mother. Therefore the eulogy was all about my mother."

Project Renewment women generally were reluctant to discuss end-of-life issues. Only after meeting for five years did one group spend an evening discussing their preferences about how they would like to spend their last days and the meaning of quality of life. And only two of the seven Renewment groups have ever discussed end-of-life subjects.

Many of our women have not purchased plots or made arrangements for burial or cremation. Few have shared their desires about how they want to live the end of their lives besides having a "do not resuscitate" order. Studies have shown that although most people believe that advanced directives are a good idea, only about 7 to 8 percent developed them.[1] We are not unlike the general population, deluding ourselves that if we don't discuss the end, it won't happen.

Acknowledging our own mortality in concrete terms can be startling and discomforting. Elisabeth Kübler-Ross's book *On Death and Dying*[2] was published in 1969, yet still the subject is avoided even among the brightest and most enlightened women and men.

The initial reactions of Renewment women to end-of-life discussions were "I don't want to live if I am out of it," or "I don't want to be kept alive in a vegetative state." These declarations are important but not sufficient. The questions we need to ask ourselves should include what we want if we face decline, and the answers should be shared with friends and family. The moment of death is simple; the dying process is not. Consequently we need to make known our desires and instructions for what we consider a good death.

Group I, the initial group started by the coauthors, used a publication entitled "Your Way: A Guide to Help You Stay in Charge of Decisions About Your Medical Care."[3] The pamphlet was useful in tackling a difficult personal subject.

Keeping the end in sight, we were able to identify what we wanted for ourselves in the different stages of decline. We identified conditions for wanting medical care, pain medication and measures to prolong life. If we were unable to communicate and near death, we identified different types of care that could be administered or withheld. Exercising the choices while we are still healthy is the key. The group consensus on the large decisions was that no one wanted a painful or lingering death. If we could depend on excellent 24–7 care and having a loving, reliable person with us who would supervise the attending staff, dying at home was preferable.

The decisions were more complicated than we assumed, and the number of details that emerged was a surprise. How do we want people to behave toward us? Do we want them to speak with us? Touch us? How do we want to be kept comfortable? The choices range from "keeping me fresh and clean" to "reading me poetry." How much pain medication do we want? Do we want to die at home? How do we feel about hospice care? Do we want to talk about our death or would we like to avoid that subject? Do we have a family that can help us to feel comfortable about dying?

We acknowledged that what we think we want in our healthy state may change if we find ourselves faced with a terminal illness or in substantial pain. Although we need to consider such difficult situations, we also must be open to changing our minds if faced with a serious condition.

Making end-of-life decisions involves a person or people who will commit to ensure our wishes are carried out. Several married women were concerned about having their husbands responsible for executing their decisions. "My husband could not carry out my wishes. It would be too emotional for him. I instead have asked my younger sister to take responsibility for orchestrating this for me. I know that she will be able to be more levelheaded."

Some women did not want to plan the details, leaving arrangements for the memorial service or funeral to the family after their deaths. In deference to our families, plans for cremation or burial are choices that are best made by us. Also, selecting and paying for a burial plot makes life easier for those we leave behind.

One woman said, "My parents bought our burial plots because they wanted to be sure we were buried next to them."

Another commented, "My husband died of a prolonged illness. He planned his memorial service, including the selection of the place, food served and speakers. It was of great relief to me that he made these decisions. I knew he got exactly what he wanted."

A gerontologist told about a phone call she received from her sister-in-law toward the end of her struggle with cancer. "She said, 'I want to be buried next to you and my brother.' I replied, 'That's fine, not to worry' and turned to my husband. 'Your sister wants to be buried next to us, and at the moment we are nowhere.' I quickly purchased three burial plots at a group rate so not only she, but we would be somewhere. My husband died one year later."

Death of a spouse was part of our discussion. "I don't think that I want to live without my husband. We do everything with each other. Life would lose meaning for me." Some of us hoped that we would die before our spouses, with some taking comfort in believing that we would be the first to exit.

The situation is different when a spouse is significantly older or sicker than we are. "Since my husband is thirteen years older and has had serious health problems, I realize that he will most likely die first. I make sure that I have a life of my own in order to maintain my independence. But I know that there is no way to adequately prepare for losing him."

An anthropologist noted that her husband had all of the serious health problems in her family. "It is most likely that he will go first. My mother was left a widow and managed well after my father's death. She and other women who have had full lives after their husbands died are my role models."

Legacy is part of the end-of-life discussion. We want to believe that we will be remembered for our accomplishments as well as for our spirit. We hope to have made a difference in the world and be remembered for those differences. A discussion about end-of-life issues is practical, considerate and a reminder to live fully and well.

Questions to ask yourself:

1. What can you do to make sure you get what you want at the end of your life? What kind of agreements (legal or otherwise) can you make with your loved ones?
2. What have you done to prepare for your funeral, burial or cremation? If you don't want to plan it, who would you like to do the planning for you?
3. What have been your thoughts and feelings regarding your death?
4. What conversations have you had with your family and close friends about your end-of-life wishes?
5. What is your legacy?

26

FOREVER GUILTY

Conscience is what hurts when everything else feels so good.

—ANONYMOUS

Guilt is a feeling we experience when we believe we have done something wrong, or have not done something well enough. It occurs when we have done too much or too little, or when we should have done something but instead, did nothing. We know that stealing and coveting one's neighbor are inherently wrong. The worst part of doing what we know is wrong is the unbearable burden of guilt that follows. Guilt keeps most of us on the straight and narrow, while sustaining careers for Jewish comedians and serving as an annuity for shrinks.

Once retired, we have all the ammunition we need to feel guilty. We feel guilty when

we sleep until 8:00 A.M.
we are still in our bathrobes at 10:00 A.M.
we spend more than twenty minutes reading the
    newspaper.
we have a glass of wine alone at 4:00 P.M.

We feel guilty when

we spend a day doing just what we feel like doing.
we don't volunteer.
we hang out at Starbucks.
we don't exercise.
we spend too much time exercising.
we eat too much.
we gain weight.

We feel guilty when

we read in the middle of the afternoon.
we get a massage in the middle of the afternoon.
we do anything but work in the middle of the
    afternoon.

We feel guilty when

we say "no."
we don't take our mother out to lunch.
we can't wait for our grandchildren to leave.
we don't take our mother to the doctor.
we don't want to listen to our children's problems.

We feel guilty when

we spend too much money.
we don't understand our financial investments.
we have no idea what a reverse annuity mortgage is.
we don't balance our checkbook.
we spend $400 on a cashmere bathrobe.
we spend $10,000 on a face-lift.
we don't contribute to good causes.
we spend $300 on a pair of shoes.
we buy a $100 skin-firming moisturizer.
we buy the diamond earrings.

We feel guilty when

we haven't bought a plot for ourselves.
we are jealous of our best friend.
we have a tummy tuck.
we forget a friend's birthday.
we forget our own anniversary.
we watch the housekeeper dust.

We feel guilty when

we don't want to drive at night.
we ask our mates to pick us up and drive us around the
    parking lot so we can find our car.
we lose our glasses.
we lose our cell phone.
we lose our favorite pen.
we can't maneuver into a parking space.

We feel guilty when

we no longer want to throw dinner parties.
we serve Cheerios for dinner.
we do take-out food three times a week.
we eat out seven days a week.

We feel guilty when

we don't spend enough time with our adult children.
we don't give enough time to our grandchildren.
we lie on the sofa all day with a cold.
we cannot drive our grandson to preschool.
we don't read political e-mails.
we are being good to ourselves.

Questions to ask yourself:

1. What person or situation made you feel guilty for the first time?
2. What recent incident made you feel guilty?
3. To what extent does guilt motivate your behavior?
4. If you feel guilty, is it related to responsibilities, regrets, obligations, shame or covering for irrational beliefs?
5. If you feel guilty, how do you alleviate these feelings?

27

SEX:
LEST WE FORGET

Sex without love is an empty experience, but as empty experiences go, it's a pretty good one.

—WOODY ALLEN

Ben Franklin got it right—more or less—in his advice to a friend battling his lustful feelings for women. In a letter, Franklin suggested marriage. Knowing that his friend would reject that solution, he suggested that his friend should have affairs with "old women," meaning women over forty-five years of age. "In your amours, you should prefer old women to young ones."[1] The reasons according to Franklin were substantial: Old women have more knowledge of the world, can carry on a good conversation and use their minds for observation. They are tender when you are sick; they eliminate the hazard of children; are prudent and discreet, which prevents suspicion; and prevent prostitutes from ruining a man's health and fortune. And finally, "They are so grateful!"[2]

Franklin further advised his friend on ways to have sex with older women. He wrote that his friend should use a basket to cover up anything exposed above a woman's "girdle." By covering her wrinkled face, neck, breasts and arms, it is difficult to tell the difference between a young one and an old one. He also recommended turning out the lights because "all cats are grey" (in the dark).[3] Franklin is known as a famous scientist, inventor, statesman, printer, philosopher, musician and economist. Fortunately, his fame was not dependent on sex instruction. And Franklin did return to his original advice: get married.

The negative views of older women and their sexuality still persist. We rarely see steamy sexy love scenes between two seventy-year-olds on movie or television screens. Older men are paired with younger women. Jack Nicholson at age sixty starred with Helen Hunt, age thirty-four, in the film As Good as It Gets. A midlife woman's victory finally occurred when Diane Keaton, at age fifty-seven, starred with Jack Nicholson, age sixty-six, in the movie Something's Got to Give. Keaton was nominated for an Academy Award for best actress and received the Golden Globe Award for best actress in a motion picture. Project Renewment women cheered. Despite these small advances, we still receive the message that the game is over for mature women. Hollywood and society couldn't be more wrong.[4]

Gail Sheehy in her book Sex and the Seasoned Woman writes about an interview with Kitty Carlisle Hart, who was one of America's grandest sirens.[5] When she was ninety-five, she was paid $20,000 to get up on a table and sing in Palm Beach. She was asked if seduction is mainly a head trip. "Yes, I think so . . . I don't know about the very young girls who have big bosoms. But to me, the real sex appeal is in the imagination. . . . And all men want to be listened to. I am a very good listener."[6]

A sixty-three-year-old legal librarian talked about her experiences. "After forty years of marriage we still have sex. It is more satisfying now than it was when we were young. Our relationship is so much deeper and we are more connected. Even if our sex life didn't continue for some reason, we would continue to have that connection."

"Sex is not just a matter of athletics and production."[7] Dr. Robert N. Butler, coauthor of *The New Love and Sex After 60*, writes that some people develop the "second language of sex."[8] It consists of being sensitive to the feelings of another person and is expressed in words, actions, tenderness and thoughtfulness. It is learned rather than instinctive and is acquired slowly and deliberately over the years through giving and taking. Some develop this language throughout their relationship. Others rely on it when they develop physical limitations affecting their sexual activities.

A fifty-eight-year-old woman added her thoughts. "I have been married for thirty-five years and had a great sex life up until my husband got a serious illness and then everything stopped. At first it was very hard for me, but I have gotten used to it. We still touch and snuggle and that feels good. I feel lucky to still have him."

Feeling that we exude sexuality is a powerful sensation. If we have been desired and admired by a man for thirty or forty years, we may miss that feeling when it is gone. Not having that intimate part of us activated can easily produce a feeling of incompleteness. "It's like being all dressed up and having no place to go."

Single women gave their perspective. "I haven't had sex in years and have lost my desire. I don't feel sensuous, because I would have to have someone touching me or holding me."

"I have been a widow for one year. I miss my husband in so many ways. I miss his companionship, the comfort of our relationship, his holding my hand and telling me that I look beautiful. And, I do miss our sex life. I would enjoy having a man for a friend, someone with whom I could have dinner or go to a movie. I just want that person to be healthy and good company. Sex is less important."

The subject of sex and sexuality was discussed by only two groups. Our sense was that women were somewhat hesitant to discuss sex, which may not be unusual for those brought up in the socially conservative period of the 1950s. One group was only comfortable discussing the subject after meeting for several years. For many the topic was a private one; bedroom performance was not for public discussion.

Our women had various thoughts and feelings about their own sexuality. For some, sex has become less important at this stage of life, attributed in part to menopause. For others, sex and intimacy have become more important and is "better than ever." Others miss the physical sexual relationship. "If I could pay for safe sex, I would. Without a man, some of me has died." Many women missed the desires and intense climaxes, the intense passion of youth and being easily aroused. Some were troubled that they never again would experience sexual passion while others felt comfortable adjusting to these changes.

Having a sexual relationship at this time of our lives can be an affirmation of our sexuality and sensuality. We can feel vital and alive with the primary or secondary language of sex. Availability of a partner plays a significant role. Those of us who never married, are single, divorced or widowed either adjust or find ways to satisfy our wants and needs. No question, this is easier said than done. When all else fails, we may need to buy a couple of AA batteries.

Questions to ask yourself:
1. How important is intimacy and a sexual relationship to you?
2. What do you think about the "second" language of sex? Have you experienced it?
3. Where do you find emotional and physical intimacy?
4. How do you feel about your sexuality?
5. How does your sexuality tie into your feelings of being attractive or unattractive?

I LOST MY KEYS AND MY CAR

You know you are getting older when . . . getting lucky means you find your car in the parking lot.

— Unknown

"It was light when I started shopping and pitch-black when I left the stores with my shopping bags. I was sure I knew where I parked the car. I pulled out my keys and pushed the unlock button on the key ring, waiting to hear the "beep" and see the blinking headlights emanating from my lost car. I saw nothing and heard silence." So were the words of an experienced Project Renewment shopper.

"I was in a rush to go to the airport for a flight to New York. The car keys . . . I knew they were somewhere in the house. What were they doing in my underwear drawer?" added another.

A sixty-eight-year-old attorney chimed in, "I was at a party with a friend whom I have known for twenty-five years. I wanted to introduce her to others. How could I have forgotten her name? Maybe I have the beginning of Alzheimer's disease."

We all forget something at some time. Yet forgetfulness worried Project Renewment women as a sign that they may be on the down slope, were losing their memories and moving to the beginning of the end. Alzheimer's disease was the ultimate fear. Just the thought of losing mental control was described as frightening, and was heightened when they coupled this with their impending transition to retirement.

The attorney continued, "Part of the reason I retired was because my job became so stressful. I was finding that I made mistakes because I couldn't remember details. I think I am just having memory problems because I am getting old."

Stress is one of many causes of memory problems. Under stress we produce higher levels of the stress hormone cortisol, which is known to impair memory.[1] Other causes of memory loss include sleep disorders, depression, infection, Vitamin B12 deficiency, alcoholism and drugs. The good news is that these causes are reversible.

We can easily become concerned if we forget an appointment or don't remember what we saw on television, confusing ordinary forgetfulness with memory loss. And we often believe our memory is worse than it is. Fortunately, our perceptions most frequently are wrong. Research studies validate the fact that our memory typically is much better than we think it is.

There are reasons we become anxious about forgetfulness that have little to do with our ability to remember things. Normal physical changes are often confused with mental changes. If we have a hearing loss or a vision problem, it is a short leap to assume that our mental abilities also are diminishing. We also are more aware of our memory failures than younger people.[2] Students often forget their books, lunches or pocket money and typically show little concern. If we experience the same forgetfulness, we may believe we have a worrisome memory problem. Combined with society's expectations that older people "mentally lose it," we can easily start to question whether we have the beginnings of dementia.

Memory is often envisioned as a large filing cabinet that stores information for later use. When the cabinet is full, it takes longer to pull up the file. Based on this assumption, individuals would have an excellent memory if they could accurately recall detailed information from past events and experiences. According to current theory and research, this approach to memory has little basis.

We have different types of memory. Short-term memory, also known as working memory, stores information we want or need to recall. An example would be conveying a telephone message or remembering to buy milk at the grocery store. Long-term memory consists of important information we want to retain such as the names of family members and addresses, and information on how to do certain activities.

There is more. Long-term memory can be divided into explicit memory—facts that we make a conscious effort to learn such as the names of our staff or the names of a construction crew working on our house. Implicit memory is information we need to carry out routine tasks such as driving a car. And semantic memory stores facts so deeply ingrained, little effort is required to recall them. The months of the year would be an example.[3]

With age, we may lose some short-term memory. Other types of memory show little if any decline with age. The good news is that the brain is more flexible and adaptable than we once thought.[4] It retains its capacity to form new memories, which means it makes new connections between the brain cells. The astounding news is that we can grow new brain cells. Equally astounding is the finding that learning plays a big role.

Just the process of learning causes physical changes in the brain. When our minds are challenged, neurons sprout new branchlike extensions called dendrites. When these extensions or dendrites come in contact with one another, they form synapses. The more dendrites our brain makes, the easier it is for brain cells to communicate with one another, promoting the exchange of information. The number, density and length of dendrites reach their greatest level from our early fifties to our late seventies. Now we know we may not have yet peaked.

Brain health is a relatively new industry based on technology, science and the exploding number of older adults. Companies have developed games and exercises to keep our brains functioning at their highest level. In September of 1996, the Nintendo store in Manhattan hosted a video competition to determine the "Coolest Grandparent." They were playing *Brain Age*, a mind-challenging game for the forty-plus group who are worried about losing their "mental edge."[5] The Brain Fitness Program, developed by Posit Science Corporation, is a computer-based set of exercises that enhance cognitive ability.

More than fifty scientists and clinicians from the United States, Europe, Asia and the Middle East created this brain fitness program. One of its goals is to stimulate brain physiology to produce brain chemicals that strengthen memory.

Dr. Gary Small, Director of the UCLA Center on Aging, has developed a memory prescription consisting of physical exercise, nutrition and "mental aerobics."[6] He notes, the plan "can lead to significant improvements in . . . memory performance in as little as two weeks."[7]

The brain workouts are based on three memory training skills. The first is to *look*, which means to slow down and actively observe what you want to learn and to pay attention to details. It relies on our five senses of look, listen, feel, taste and smell. An example is how we use our memory for street directions. When driving, we are likely to remember the directions. As a passenger on the first trip, we likely won't recall the directions when driving to the same destination.[8] Lack of attention is the likely reason.

The second part of the brain workout is *snap*, which is creating mental snapshots of memories. The snaps can be real or imagined. The type of snapshots best remembered are bright, colorful, involve movement, are three-dimensional and detailed. For example, when parking the car on level 3B, one could develop a mental image of 3B. Dr. Small visualizes the "image of three bumblebees hovering over my car."[9] Since he has an aversion to bees, he remembers the image. Others may visualize three bears sitting in their car because their children loved stories about bears.[10]

The third component is *connect,* which links mental snapshots together. It is useful in putting together names and faces, names of employee's spouses and birth dates. The technique includes placing one image on another, merging the images or wrapping the images around one another. Another way to use *connect* is to create words from the first letters of what you want to remember. Many of us used this system in school to memorize presidents or the fifty states.

The question remains: "When is it time to worry about memory loss?" If we ask the same question repeatedly, can no longer follow a recipe or become lost on familiar streets, it may be time to make an appointment with a geriatrician, neurologist or other professional specializing in the diseases and health of older adults. Depending on the cause, we will probably find that our symptoms are temporary and reversible.

An older Mark Twain reflected on his memory as a youth. "When I was younger I could remember anything, whether it happened or not. . . ."[11]

Questions to ask yourself:

1. If you have noticed changes in your memory, under what circumstances do these occur?
2. How do you feel when you cannot remember something?
3. What do you do when you can't remember something that is important to you?
4. How does your short-term memory compare to your long-term memory?
5. What is your brain fitness program?

29

PUSHING SIXTY

When I feel like exercising, I just lie down until the feeling goes away.

—Robert M. Hutchins

Age sixty is not the time to stop moving. If we do, it is likely that our breasts will surrender to gravity, our posteriors will drop, the flesh under our chins will likely flap in the breeze, and skin from our upper arms will droop. Add to that muscle flabbiness, a curvy spine, weight gain and heavy breathing while we walk around the block. Such changes are part of normal aging and can be postponed with one simple commitment—regular exercise.

During our working years, time was scarce. Exercise was what many of us did with extra time. And the StairMaster we received for the holidays was used to hang our hand-washed laundry on. Some of us did exercise. We took our walking shoes to work, got up at 5:00 A.M. to go to the gym, went to Pilates on Saturday morning or jogged at 7:00 P.M. with blinking lights on our shoes and vest.

Whether working or not, women in Project Renewment agreed that physical and mental fitness is extremely important. Many walk, jog, cycle, swim, ski and play golf and tennis. Others do yoga, tai chi, weightlifting, hiking and Pilates. In this new phase of life, we are likely to have more control of our time and consequently more opportunity to exercise on a regular basis—if we choose to.

"It takes me half the day to do my exercises, shower and get dressed," says one woman committed to exercise. She goes on to say, "It is important that I feel I am master of my own body. I am grateful that everything is still working, although I am aware that my body is not what it was thirty-five years ago."

A sixty-five-year-old woman talked about her mishap. "I decided to join my grandson while he was ice skating. After five minutes on the ice I wanted to show him how I made a turn. I slipped and shattered my wrist. I guess I'm not thirteen anymore." Some caution is in order. With age, we are more at risk for sports injuries. Such injuries among Baby Boomers increased 33 percent between 1991 and 1998.[1]

Exercise is an effective intervention to slow the normal aging process. We know that with age we lose lean muscle tissue and gain fat tissue. Muscle loss means we lose strength that affects balance, posture and in some cases the ability to live independently.

But studies have shown that men and women can build muscle mass well into their eighties. Even those in their nineties who are frail from inactivity can double their strength. For some that means getting out of a chair independently or progressing from a walker to a cane.[2]

The National Institute on Aging suggests four types of exercise that will improve our health and abilities.

Endurance exercises: Exercises such as jogging, cycling, speed walking and swimming increase breathing and heart rate, and improve our circulatory system and the health of our lungs. Imagine climbing to the top of the Eiffel Tower or chasing after your two-year-old grandchild with plenty of breath to spare.

Strength exercises: Pilates and resistance training build muscle strength, prevent osteoporosis and keep weight down, helping to prevent diabetes and other health problems. Imagine lifting your ten-month-grandchild out of the high chair and into the playpen or being able to move the large trash bin to the curb for pickup.

Balance exercises: Yoga and Pilates can improve balance and prevent falling, a significant problem among older adults and the major cause of broken hips and other injuries that can lead to disability and dependency. Imagine standing erect and being stable in all that you do.

Flexibility exercises: Stretching in an exercise, yoga, ballet or Pilates class can keep us limber. As part of the normal aging process, connective tissues get tighter and can limit our range of motion. Stretching keeps us flexible, helps prevent falls and allows us to dance the night away.

Walking is an exercise that includes most of these elements. Almost everyone can do it, and no gym membership or athletic equipment is required. Walking can slow the decline of aging by building endurance, improving muscle tone, increasing joint flexibility and strengthening bones.[3] It has a low potential for injury and helps in weight loss, and can prevent or control heart disease, hypertension and other diseases.[4]

Many of our women have walking groups. "I have walked with the same group of friends for the past twenty years. It is our walk and talk therapy." Experts agree that the number one contributor to maintaining a regular exercise program is that we like our regimen and the people with whom we exercise. Evidence suggests that when we exercise with others, we tend to stick to our routine better than when we do it alone.

Exercise is easy to avoid. We are too busy and don't like to sweat. The outdoor temperature is too cold or too hot. If we feel fine and look good, why bother? We know Mary, Jack or Sarah who died at 102 and never exercised. We hate going to the gym where our flabby muscles will stand out among those young, firm, semi-naked bodies on the exercise machines.

Certain environments can be disincentives for exercising. For those who do not want to work out with the spandex set, niche gyms have emerged, growing from about two facilities ten years ago to a few hundred today.[5] Nifty After Fifty, Club 50 Fitness and Silver Sneakers offer fitness programs to adults who may have less than perfectly toned bodies. Curves, Bally Total Fitness and Gold's Gym also are incorporating fitness programs for the mature set.[6]

"When my husband was battling cancer, he used a walker and then a wheelchair. In caring for him, I exerted an enormous amount of energy in assisting him, making it appear effortless. I was grateful I could do so. There is no question that my Pilates and yoga classes allowed me to be the best I could be both physically and emotionally."

Given that two-thirds of adults don't exercise regularly,[7] we need well-researched and validated reasons to remind us of the significance of exercise. The National Institute on Aging provides us with the following motivation:[8]

- Evidence indicates that a lack of physical activity combined with poor nutrition is the second greatest underlying cause of death in the United States. Smoking is the number one cause.
- Exercise can help people feel better and get more enjoyment out of life.
- Exercise can prevent or delay the onset of some diseases such as cancer, heart disease or diabetes.
- Exercise can increase energy and often counteracts depression.
- Exercise and activity help increase chances to remain independent.

The final motivator is evidence that exercise can extend life expectancy.

Telomeres, which are chunks of DNA at the ends of each chromosome, get shorter with age. "When there are no telomeres left, we start to die."[9] Exercise extends telomeres and therefore may extend life.

Some may subscribe to the philosophy of Mark Twain, who said, "I'm pushing sixty. That is enough exercise for me."[10] May this philosophy be a passing thought.

Questions to ask yourself:

1. What kind of activities do you like to do? Which of them involve movement?
2. How would you describe your commitment to and discipline to exercise?
3. What motivates you to exercise? What stops you?
4. What forms of exercise would you like to try?
5. Do you know of others with whom you could exercise?

30

LOSING A MATE

*A man's dying is more the survivor's affair
than his own.*

—THOMAS MANN

"I just feel numb. It doesn't feel real to me. It's as though he has gone on a business trip and will soon be coming home. I am still waiting." These are the words of a recent widow in Project Renewment.

The death of a husband is an incomprehensible life-altering experience. It is one of the "most emotionally difficult and taxing experiences in anyone's lifetime."[2] It takes time to fully comprehend such a loss. Some of us are able to move on to develop new relationships while cherishing memories of those we have lost. Others struggle with that loss throughout their lives.

"Although we never made specific plans for our retirement, we just assumed we would grow old together and have a grand time doing it. He had been ill for five years, yet it was a shock when he died," said another. Few of us are fully prepared for that moment of stunning loss, that moment when we realize we will face the future without him. Yet, it happens—particularly since women, on average, live five years longer than men.

After her husband's death, a Project Renewment woman felt she could only be with people with whom she felt good. "These people who I felt comfortable with experienced loss themselves, or if they had not, they were not afraid of death. Some friends would come and spend the night with me. It was comforting to have another person with me in an otherwise empty house. I am forever grateful to friends who brought food. I was unable to cook and eating was difficult."

All religions and cultures have their own rituals and customs around death: when to be buried; where to be buried; having a wake, a closed or open casket, a funeral or memorial service, food after the funeral, condolence visits and sitting shiva. There is no universal protocol on how to comfort the bereaved.

A group of recent widows and widowers distinguished the difference between effective and irrelevant expressions of solace. They developed some "dos and don'ts" for offering condolences to women (and men) who recently lost their partners.[3] Here are some of their recommendations.

- Stay in touch: send e-mails, make telephone calls and send greeting cards for different holidays. "Just thinking of you" goes a long way.
- Be the planner/initiator. Instead of asking, "What do you want to do? Say "I'll pick you up at 5:00 and we'll go to Emilio's café for dinner."
- Be honest. Say, "I don't really know how you feel. I just want

you to know that I will always be here for you." And then make sure you are present for that person.

- Share dinners. Suggest a potluck so you are the company for dinner. Days can become very lonely, particularly at mealtime.
- Give a hug. A warm and caring embrace provides a wonderful feel-good moment.
- Give permission. Tell her it is okay to talk about her husband. And shedding a tear or two is equally acceptable.
- Suggest overnight company. Ask her if she would like a houseguest for the night. This helps fill a void . . . at least for an evening.

We are advised to avoid these well-intended phrases.

- "I really know how you feel."
- "He is better off."
- "Are you dating yet?"
- "You'll get over it."
- "You just need to keep busy."
- "With such a big house you really should move."
- "You're young," implying "you always can remarry."

As we age, the number of men and women we know facing life-threatening illnesses increase. Perhaps we all are living in a decade of personal vulnerability just because we are getting older. Illnesses and losses experienced by our family and friends whom we love remind us of the fine line we all travel. Such losses can serve as a wake-up call. They stimulate us to think about whether we are spending our time in ways that are best for us. Such wake-up moments can serve as pristine opportunities to create a life of meaning, fulfillment and, yes, even joy.

Widows have done it. They have seized the moment and made it work for them. Some embark on travel, immerse in gourmet cooking, spend more time with grandchildren, paint, write or take leadership roles in organizations. The journey is not easy. If there is anything we have learned throughout our careers and lives, it is that nothing of importance is simple or easily accomplished.

Even with satisfying activities and relationships, women who have lost their beloved mates still have deep fears and trepidations. In addition to financial concerns, they fear growing old alone. They are faced with this reality while others speculate, never believing deep down that they can face the future as a single older woman.

Project Renewment was never intended to be a support group. Yet it became an extraordinary supportive unit of women to those in the grips of dealing with the deaths of their husbands or their own life-threatening illnesses. Our women found ways they could be most helpful because they knew one another on a deep, personal level and consequently, knew how best to offer solace.

Life is a gift. Most of us have experienced the pain when that gift is taken from a loved one. Although grief is part of the recovery process, we know that widows do get better and can, once again, live life to the fullest. We in Project Renewment have seen it. A new sense of identity, a renewed view of the future, and taking risks to do something different are possibilities and realities.

As widows, we have more time for ourselves and can explore and create that new chapter in our lives. We can believe that there still are peak experiences in store for us. The brass ring has never moved. It still is there for the taking—when we are ready.

Questions to ask yourself:

1. What have you learned about yourself as a mourner?
2. What has provided you the most comfort in times of mourning?
3. What can you do to prepare for a potential and profound loss?
4. How would you comfort a woman who lost her husband?
5. What deaths have affected you most, and why?

31

HONORING OUR WISDOM

Knowledge is a process of piling up facts;
wisdom lies in their simplification.

—Martin Fischer

Walgreens, with its more than five thousand pharmacy and convenience stores in forty-six states, is willing to pay for wisdom. In partnership with AARP in 2007, they are actively recruiting capable and mature people as employees with a clear message on their website—"Now Hiring your Wisdom."[1]

In an era that values technology, speed, deliverables and immediate returns on investments, wisdom may seem irrelevant. Yet we know that tapping knowledge and experience can forge new directions, prevent new problems and solve current or old ones. For example, in 1986 after the space shuttle *Challenger* disaster, NASA promptly contacted a select group of experienced retired scientists to determine what went wrong. Their wisdom was highly valued.

Wisdom typically is not a trait listed on a job description with good reason. It is hard to identify and measure, and difficult to find consensus in its meaning. The most accepted definition of wisdom is the accumulation of knowledge and experience. Since we have to live long enough to acquire both, age is a third element.

Wisdom is "the ability to exercise good judgment on important, but uncertain matters," a definition used by President Jimmy Carter.[2] It is a product of "age, smarts, emotional and practical life experience."[3] It allows us to respond to complex situations with more than one answer, integrating our thinking and feeling, and our hearts and minds.[4] Wisdom reminds us that there is no situation without hope, and that time is a powerful healer.[5]

Wisdom can grow as we age. It is the cumulative consolidation of all of life's experiences and lessons that teach us how to prioritize, know what really matters and how to share it with others. It is directed to the long-term good,[6] yet focuses on the past as well as the future.[7] It is the ability to "discern truth and exercise good judgment."[8]

Wisdom also is connected to physiology. The brain process is fundamental because wisdom relies on memory, both old and new memories, emotional and intellectual ones as well as verbal and nonverbal ones.[9] Although some brain cells decline with age, our storage capacity for memories has no known limits,[10] and our degree of wisdom has no boundaries.

Wisdom has personal meaning. Here are some impressions and thoughts about wisdom from our Project Renewment women. "When I feel wise I am very much in the present. I feel centered and calm. It is a spiritual feeling."

"I lose touch with my wisdom when I am not feeling good about myself. At those times I don't feel as if I have anything to offer to anyone."

"I asked my ninety-one-year-old mother what she learned from life. Her response was 'listen and keep your mouth shut.'"

Perhaps "wisdom is the reward you get for a lifetime of listening when you'd have preferred to talk."[11]

"If I consciously try to be less judgmental and display kindness to people, it will contribute to my becoming a wiser person."

A retired executive attending a cocktail party was asked what she did. Instead of saying she used to be a product manager, she replied, "I employ the wisdom that I have spent my entire life gathering." If you use such a statement, be prepared for at least three responses: silence, "what do you mean by that?" or the person moving on to chat with someone else. Wisdom is not an easy subject to discuss, particularly in a crowd, with a martini in hand.

A teacher commented, "I grew up in a time when we were silent about what we didn't know. It was a time in which we had to be uniformly excellent. We thought a wise person was an expert and infallible." Now most of us know that even wise people make mistakes and can recognize their shortcomings with confidence.

When we acknowledge our gifts and figure out a way to maximize them for ourselves and in our relationships with others, we are wise. Wisdom is a unique benefit that accompanies experience and remains with us. It enables us to probe deep inside ourselves and to be comfortable with where we are in our lives. Wisdom depicts a phase of life characterized by "knowing who we are inside and believing that what we are doing is a true reflection and expression of our genuine self."[12]

Wisdom allows us to mentor and lead. Sharing thoughts and experiences on ethical issues, organizational mazes and how to make the best of one's talents comes from years of experience. Wisdom is an attitude that goes beyond "been there, done that." It's extrapolating the messages and lessons learned from life experiences that allow us to pass on the legacies of wisdom to others.

Despite the varied definitions of wisdom, several themes are clear. Knowledge is a basis for wisdom. Wise individuals do not act on impulse; they know better. Wise people have the ability to interpret knowledge, and that knowledge can come from books or experience. To be wise, individuals need to have opportunities for growth and creativity. The cornerstone of wisdom is experience. That, combined with introspection, reflection and intuition, is what allows us to become wise women.

Walgreens cannot go wrong by hiring wise people. There is no doubt they will get a return on their investment. Wise employees will leave their handprints on all that they touch.

Mark Twain provided us with an appreciation of wisdom at a young age. "When I was a boy of fourteen, my father was so ignorant I could hardly stand to have the old man around. But when I got to twenty-one, I was astonished at how much he had learned in seven years."[13]

Questions to ask yourself:

1. When do you feel wise?
2. How do you use your wisdom?
3. When do you ignore your wisdom?
4. Who are the wise people in your life?
5. In what areas of your life would you like to be wiser?

32

THE ILLUSION OF FREEDOM

Freedom is that instant between when someone tells you to do something and when you decide how to respond.

—JEFFREY BORENSTEIN

No more deadlines, reorganizations, new management or the wear and tear of business travel. "I will finally be able to sleep, breathe and not hyperventilate. I might even need fewer massages and visits to my shrink."

Life on our terms has an appeal. The children are grown, the pet hamsters are gone and we look forward to "My Time."[1] As we revel in the fantasy of freedom, the miracles of medicine, healthy lifestyles and seat belts are giving us more years of life than at any other time in history. What a victory, a gift we embrace for ourselves and our loved ones.

We easily delude ourselves into believing that now we will be the centerpiece. Not yet. It is our loved ones who quickly move into that position: our aging parents.

A businesswoman said, "When the children were out of my hair, I believed that it finally was my time—time I could devote to growing the business before I retired. I was completely surprised when my mother needed help. She no longer could drive and burned the toast. She required a lot of time and I found myself becoming anxious and depressed. It seemed unfair. Eventually my mother went to an assisted living facility. Even though I wasn't delivering the immediate care, she didn't get the care she deserved unless I was present."

Parents age—some well and some not so well.

"My mother was my father's caregiver during the last ten years of his life. He resented anyone who was brought in to help with his care. He would fire them or throw a tantrum when someone new was employed. He became difficult to handle as he had a number of strokes that changed his personality. We were as concerned about my mother as we were about my father. I tried to be of help to my mother, but I had young children so my time was limited. Twenty-five years later my mother needs care and I am torn between my mother and my grandchildren and fear that history will repeat itself."

Regardless of our relationship with our parents, the responsibilities are clear and feelings often conflicted.

Women talked about their experiences as caregivers. "My mother was far from being a good mother. We didn't resolve our issues before she developed Alzheimer's disease. As a child I felt abandoned by her because she did not intervene when my father verbally abused me. At this point in my life I have forgiven her, but I must admit that seeing to her care feels like a burden."

"My sister and I both work full-time, one on the East Coast and the other on the West Coast. We share the care of my father, who lives in Florida. She does all of the administrative work; I do all of the hands-on work. I feel I have the heavier end of the bargain."

"I grew up with my grandmother living with my parents and us children. That was common in my day. But should the time come when my mother can no longer live independently, I could not have her live with us."

Caregiving is a serious responsibility. It also can be a time to capture precious moments of love, honesty, meaning and healing.

A retired businesswoman shared the following story: "The year I spent caring for my father-in-law was a gift I will treasure forever. It was a special time for both of us. We talked of many things, including life, death and dying. He had all of his faculties but knew he was losing control. One of my goals was to help him retain his dignity. He was dressed and shaved every day. And I helped him bathe. He felt too embarrassed to ask his son. The role reversal was more than he could take. A goal for 'Dad' was to have a daily purpose and destination. When cooking, he helped me with the string beans; when doing laundry, he helped fold. Each morning he would awake and say, 'Honey, what's on the agenda today?' We had one outing—every day. We would go to the library. He would select books and never read them. But that was okay. We went to Vons with his wheelchair and he held the groceries. I also got him a cat, even though I am allergic to cats. I thought he needed something to cuddle and hold and to take care of to the best of his ability."

Caregiving can be "a gift in disguise"[2]—an experience that moves us toward a more meaningful connection with ourselves and others.[3] "Being close to my mother at the end of her life was a blessing and a testament to our relationship and the joy we had together during all of the years I was growing up," said one woman.

A gerontologist commented, "I traveled frequently to Florida to be with my ninety-three-year-old father in his last months of suffering from lung cancer. I received a telephone call. He said he loved me. In my fifty-seven years of life, I had never heard that before."

As women, we provide the majority of care for aging parents.[4] Gender equality is not part of caregiving. The typical caregiver is a forty-six-year-old woman who is married and working.[5] Recently, men have assumed greater responsibility by providing 40 percent of the care.[6] Overall, though, women still give more hours of care and a higher level of care than their male counterparts.[7]

Many women in Project Renewment were facing retirement when they were confronted with elder care challenges. Among a group of ten women, six were providing care for their elderly mothers or in-laws. Five of these mothers died over a five-year period. Three developed Alzheimer's disease or some form of dementia at the end of their lives. Project Renewment women gave care and support in all of these cases.

To face caregiving alone can be overwhelming. Caregivers and authors Cappy Capossela and Sheila Warnock developed a creative approach to sharing responsibility, information and work. They created a model to form caregiving families composed of friends and acquaintances of someone who is seriously ill. Their premise is that you don't have to do it alone. In their book *Share the Care: How to Organize a Group to Care for Someone Who Is Seriously Ill*,[8] they describe ways to create these special families.

The emotional and physical toll of caregiving is high. Family caregivers are considered the most neglected group in the health and long-term care industry.[9] They use prescription drugs for depression, anxiety and insomnia two to three times as often as the rest of the population.[10]

Caregiving also is a business decision with bottom-line implications.[11] The cost nationally to U.S. employers is up to $33.6 billion a year, taking into account costs for replacement, absenteeism, workday interruptions, supervision, unpaid leave and reduced hours. Employers can calculate the cost of elder care by plugging in just three figures into an on-line calculator: the size of the business, the average hourly wage and the estimated number of employed caregivers.[12] Perhaps the costs will motivate more employers to provide elder care services of flextime, home-care resources and other supportive services.

It is likely that each one of us will be affected by caregiving at some point in our lives. Rosalynn Carter said it well. "There are only four kinds of people in this world: those who *have been* caregivers, those who currently *are* caregivers, those who *will be* caregivers and those who *will need* caregivers." That does include all of us.[13]

We know that freedom from work does not free us from responsibility, obligation or duty. Most of our lives we have risen above the calls to duty. In the same spirit as reaching for the gold ring, we can reach to create the finest relationship with our aging parents by embracing the responsibility with love, caring and the wise use of supportive services for our loved ones and for ourselves.

Questions to ask yourself:
1. If you are a caregiver, how do you feel about it?
2. What resources are available to you in helping with providing care?
3. How do you take care of yourself while caregiving?
4. What are your great concerns regarding caregiving?
5. Who will be there for you?

33

CONNECTING TO MY SOUL

I simply believe that some part of the human self
or soul is not subject to the laws of time and space.

—CARL JUNG

Spirituality is not a workplace priority. Yet a small minority believes our souls are the source of productivity and creativity in the workplace.[1] Ian Mitroff and Elizabeth Denton, in their book *A Spiritual Audit of Corporate America*, comment that spirituality, as the sacred aspect of daily life and the source of meaning, may be the ultimate competitive advantage and one of the most important determinants of an organization's performance.[2] Nonetheless, companies usually consider spiritual issues too personal or inappropriate for the workplace.[3] Spirituality gets placed "on hold" as many of us park our souls at the door before entering the office, laboratory, courtroom, clinic or classroom.

A sixty-nine-year-old therapist gave her perspective. "I've never had time to go inward. Now that I am older and close to retirement it's time to develop another part of me, my soul, the spiritual side of myself." These words are typical of many career women facing retirement and not unusual for those entering midlife. It seems timely to explore inner feelings, to determine the meaning of our existence and our relationship to the universe. It is probably no coincidence that the Navajos and kabbalists believe that a person needs to be around forty to seriously study spirituality.[4]

Many Project Renewment women yearn to develop the spiritual part of themselves, regardless of their religious affiliations or beliefs. They want to get in touch with their "true me." Women shared their ideas of how to embark on a spiritual path.

- Learn to meditate by taking a class or working with a meditation coach.
- Attend retreats with spiritual leaders who may interest you.
- Read books and listen to tapes on spirituality. These can be found in libraries and bookstores.
- Attend classes on spirituality at colleges or universities in your local area.
- Locate websites on spirituality.
- Speak with friends about their practices.
- Form a group composed of people who want to explore spirituality with you.
- Talk to your clergyperson about the spiritual practices in your religion.
- Feel free to explore every approach until you find the one(s) that work best for you.

How and when career women find that spiritual presence varies from person to person. Here are some comments from our women about their journey.

"When I was young I thought I could find spirituality by following the gurus of the seventies. Now that I am older I know that spirituality has to come from me. Giving to my community fulfills part of my spiritual mission." Others speak about their feelings and strengths. "Being in touch with my soul makes me authentic. I find myself moving to the next level, going beyond the intellectual plain."

Other women spoke of their experiences. "I think about spirituality in terms of inner strength, the inner resources we have to achieve balance and harmony that allow us to live and deal with the issues in our lives." "Being a spiritual person means being able to transcend. I want to be able to function from the highest place possible." "I am in a spiritual place when I am living with an open heart and a nonjudgmental mind." "I feel spiritual when I no longer need to feel in control. This is when I just let the universe happen."

According to the Zen master, monk and poet Thich Nhat Hanh,[5] it is enough to live mindfully, to slow down and just enjoy each step and each breath. For high-driving professional women, this is no easy task. Adjectives such as energetic, effective and successful describe these women. They are doers. To move from "doing" to "being" is a challenge and an opportunity that may feel like a train coming to a screeching halt.

Although each person's sense of spirituality is unique, most share a common characteristic—experiencing moments of clarity that transcend the mundane.

"I felt a spiritual moment of hope when the priest laid his hands on my head when I had cancer for the second time. It was electric." "When I was praying at the wall in Jerusalem, I placed my small piece of paper with a prayer in the crack in the wall. At that moment, I connected with history." "When my husband died and my children and I were at his bedside as he took his last breath, a wind blew from the room—and out through the open window. Perhaps it was his soul or spirit that left at that moment." Those who experience such moments of enlightenment know it.

Physical environments provide a setting for spiritual experiences. For example, nature sets a stage to transcend the ordinary. Endless beauty creates moments that are timeless, serving as a catalyst for awareness and heightened senses. Smells are more intense and the sounds and silence are new. "I feel spiritual, above it all when I am on the peak of Mount Hoffman in Yosemite, looking down in the valley and wondering if life at ten thousand feet is the real world." Music has transcendental qualities. "When listening to the chorale of Beethoven's ninth symphony, I feel I am being lifted toward heaven."

Spiritual moments can occur when thinking about loved ones who have died. Their memories can make us feel connected; their souls can be a source of comfort and strength.

Women have sacrificed their souls in the name of achievement. Maureen Murdock in her book *The Heroine's Journey*[6] describes these women: "Our heroine puts on her armor, picks up her sword, chooses her swiftest steed and goes into battle. She finds her treasure: an advanced degree, a corporate title, money (or) authority. The men smile, shake her hand, and welcome her to the club." Many women have placed most if not all of their energy into a male model of success, leaving them depleted and eventually asking, "Now what?"

Our sense of spirituality can be discovered, rediscovered and strengthened with time, reflection and exploration. In a sense, our soul can be invigorated and given new life.

Developing our spiritual selves may require a shift in values. Materialism, success and social achievement may become less appealing, unimportant or even insufficient. Such values do not always meet the needs of the soul.[7] Despite the complexities, many of us want to begin an experiential quest to find greater meaning for our lives. The time and effort it takes to develop new dimensions, a new balance and a peaceful part of us is worth the journey.

Questions to ask yourself:

1. How do you feel when people start to talk about spirituality?
2. How would you describe one or more of your spiritual moments?
3. Do you have time to be reflective? If not, what has to be in place for that to occur?
4. What are the required conditions for you to be in touch with your spiritual side?
5. Is religion part of your sense of spirituality? If yes, how can you make your religion work for you to define, clarify or enhance your sense of spirituality?

34

I CAN LEAVE MY HOUSE, BUT NOT MY HAIRDRESSER

There's no place like home.

—DOROTHY IN *The Wizard of Oz*

"Color, shampoo, cut and blow-dry" are familiar routines performed by our hairdressers. After years of a "hair relationship," we no longer have to describe our desired look to them. They just know. The thought of finding a new stylist in another city, town or village can disrupt our routine and rhythm of getting things done.

Giving up our hairdresser is just one of the changes that are part of a move. To relocate means to give up the familiar, those aspects of life that have become routine for us. Without thinking we know where to buy the freshest produce, the pharmacy that has the best service and prices, and the stores where we can buy that special gift.

A communications officer for a nonprofit organization spoke about her move. "Every year for forty years, we vacationed in our favorite town located in an area that was a stark contrast to the fast-paced, congested city where we were living. We talked about retiring to our haven, but when it came time to make the move we were scared. Once we both retired, we decided to spend six weeks in our dream community to get a sense of what it would be like to live there as opposed to vacationing there. After four weeks we knew we found the perfect place and purchased a house on an acre of land. Every day we wake up feeling grateful that we don't have to leave to go home. We miss our friends and I haven't been able to get a good haircut anywhere around here. But we love our new life."

Women in Project Renewment told their stories about moving within their cities and out of state. Each story has a lesson to be learned. Each story is unique.

"As a single woman I wanted to be closer to my daughter and my new granddaughter. Since my daughter worked full-time, I knew she could use my help caring for her little one. In turn, I took comfort in knowing that I would be close to family should I face a time when I need some assistance. Also, I wanted to sever my ties with the agency I founded. Members of the staff would continuously ask for my advice and I realized that I had to distance myself from them to avoid undermining the new director. The community is ideal for me with its concentration of artists and theater, both of which I love."

"We took a long time to make the decision to move. We met with our financial adviser, who helped us make decisions about what we could afford. We interviewed several Realtors and found a married couple with whom we felt compatible. Then our house sold in twenty minutes and we had a sixty-day escrow. Fortunately, we quickly found a new place we liked. The one mistake we made was the decision to live in our new home while the remodeling was taking place. We both developed bronchial problems from inhaling all of the dust."

"After our experience I would advise people who move to plan it carefully. Be sure that your decision is financially and emotionally feasible. Think about how far you will have to drive from your new home to your favorite destinations. Avoid stairs at all cost. Even though you may be able to climb them today, you may not be able to at some time in the future."

"I was surprised at the stress involved with moving. We have moved seven times in the past twelve years and every time we move I forget how difficult it is. Now we are older and have less stamina. I would advise anyone who is moving to get the best mover possible. This is not a place to cut back on expenses."

"We made the decision to continue working rather than retire. Our house was too far from our offices and the drive to and from work became more difficult as traffic became more congested and we got older. Selling the house we built and leaving loved ones were some of the hardest decisions we ever had to make. We were fortunate to find a good-sized condominium with a panoramic view seven minutes from our offices. My one regret is that we did not get rid of more stuff before moving. There were too many things I felt I could not live without. Hiring a decorator to help us figure out our space needs would probably have been a good decision."

"My husband is twelve years older than I and the probability he will predecease me is very likely. I don't want to have to make a move by myself. I would rather sell my house and downsize to a smaller condominium that would work for us and for me alone. I also would like to live where I can walk to businesses. I get more and more nervous about driving and would like to be less dependent on my car."

"It was a desire to change our quality of life. For us, that meant living in a smaller community, close to nature, with no traffic and no pollution. I realize how important it is to me to live somewhere that represents beauty before I die."

"My husband and I were very involved with our religious community for forty years. In planning for our move, we asked our pastor to connect us with a church in the new city. Those initial welcoming contacts were invaluable, but not sufficient. Even with these new people in our lives, it dawned on us that we didn't really matter to anyone. So we did a big outreach and entertained more in six months than we did in the past twenty years. It worked."

Moving is not for everyone. Nationally, between 1995 and 2000, more than 90 percent of those sixty years and older remained in their homes or moved within the same county.[1] Reasons given for not moving were valuing ties to the community, family and friends, having had positive life experiences and the finances to stay. Dr. Robert Butler, former director of the National Institute on Aging writes, "The best place to retire is the neighborhood where you spent your life."[2] This may not be true for everyone, but it is a consideration.

The important message for all of us is to plan and think through the decision. Condominiums, smaller homes in the same neighborhood, moving permanently to a vacation home or modern retirement community are options for some of us. We also need to think about how we adapt to change. Can we live happily without our hairdresser?

Questions to ask yourself:

1. What would motivate you to move? Here are some reasons for you to review.

- Living closer to your children and grandchildren
- Needing less physical space and possessions
- Financial benefits
- Increased availability of medical services
- Greater opportunity for a more desirable lifestyle
- For health reasons and better health care
- Wanting a better climate
- Opportunities for recreational facilities
- Being closer to nature
- Having employment opportunities

2. What kind of investigating have you done to help you decide whether or not to move?
3. How can you know if a new location will work for you? Can you spend some time living there? Can you live there at different seasons of the year?
4. How do you feel about leaving your home?
5. How do you feel about leaving your friends and family?

35

JOY

Joy is the feeling of grinning inside.

—Melba Colgrove

Joy has been around a long time. In the 1960s and 1970s, we prepared meals from the *Joy of Cooking;*[1] we washed dishes with "Joy" the dishwashing liquid; and enhanced our sexual prowess by reading *The Joy of Sex.*[2] We have listened to the fourth movement of Beethoven's ninth symphony, "Ode to Joy," and people live in Joy, a city in Illinois with a population of 373.[3]

In its simplest form the word is easy to define. It is an "emotion evoked by well-being or success" synonymous with "gaiety, bliss, happiness and delight."[4] Women in Project Renewment defined joy with greater emotion than the dictionary approach. Joy was more than being happy or satisfied; it was an emotion of intensity.

"Joy is an unrestrained ecstasy; a childlike sense of awe and discovery; a visceral response." "It's a period of heightened awareness, and comes in fleeting moments that capture an instant in time."

Joy is considered close to a high that gives us a feeling of tremendous pleasure and satisfaction. Although studies have been conducted on age and joy/happiness, such feelings usually are not associated with aging. More often, aging is perceived as a downer, a period of time with inevitable declines leading to illness, fragility, impotence, dementia and losing the zip of one's spirit. Project Renewment women rejected these ageist stereotypes.

We believe and know that women in midlife and beyond have the capacity, more than ever, to have peak experiences that evoke unadulterated joy; moments that are treasured. The extent to which we allow ourselves to experience joy may depend on having sufficient time at our life stage. One woman recalled the following experience with her eighty-year-old father.

"My father was visiting from Florida. He was looking out of our picture window for a long time, first admiring a deep red cardinal and then a yellow finch feeding her young in the nest. He said to me, 'Look at these exquisite birds and the mother with her chicks,' which was followed by, 'Oh that's right, you don't have time for such things.' Besides feeling guilty, I realized that my father had the time to savor the moment and I did not. I wondered if he chose to have the time or if it was a result of just being eighty years old, knowing that he was living the later part of his life. I know at age thirty-five, I did not have the time with two young children, a career, a husband and my father as a houseguest."

For many of us, work has brought us joy and many moments to savor. Accomplishments and recognition have made our feelings soar. Such achievements among Project Renewment women included launching a small nonprofit organization to national recognition;

being recognized as one of the twenty top performers in a large bank; winning a legal case and producing a prize-winning television show.

A public relations woman looked at the other side of joy. "To be realistic, not every day at the office was joyous. Some of my workdays were totally devoid of joy. I traveled twenty-two days a month. Now in my Renewment phase of life, I feel joy when I get up in the morning and have the choice to do what makes me the happiest."

Joy was the emotion described by our women when they listened to music, saw great works of art or attended an outstanding play or film. Others loved looking at a bank of white clouds, hearing the croaking of a frog, listening to birds or being outside in the daylight. One woman felt joy when medication relieved her pain. Joy came with a good belly laugh, sexual intimacy as well as close physical relationships.

And then there were the grandchildren—holding the newborn grandbaby, the touch of that soft skin, the first smile, the "I miss you," planting a garden together and the snuggles, hugs and kisses. For grandmas, the list of joys was never ending.

Some women in Project Renewment did not relate to the experience of joy and described their emotions in a less intense way, such as pleasure or happiness. "I don't know if I ever will feel joy again." Intrusions of psychic or physical pain, stress, inertia, busyness and the "shoulds" can prevent us from having new experiences that could bring us the feeling of joy.

Nonetheless, most women in Project Renewment believe we can exercise the choice to feel joyous emotions. Given the complexity of life, we may need to compartmentalize our thoughts and experiences to create the "psychological space" needed to enjoy the moment. Yoga and meditation can help us focus and value the present, increasing the opportunity for such experiences.

Someone said, "Life is not a dress rehearsal." When we know we are temporary, as are our experiences, joy can become more intense as we age. At our life stage, we strive to have the wisdom to create and savor the joyous precious moments that are elements of a good and memorable life.

Questions to ask yourself:

1. What are some of the most joyous moments in your life?
2. What kinds of things take the joy out of your life?
3. To what extent do you currently experience joy?
4. How does aging impact your ability to experience joy?
5. What can you do to create greater joy in your days and weeks?

36

WITH A LITTLE HELP FROM MY FRIENDS

A friend may well be . . . the masterpiece of nature.

—Ralph Waldo Emerson

And for women this masterpiece is central to our lives.

Project Renewment was not designed to provide new friends for career women. But it happened. The explanation is reflected in the title of a book by Ellen Goodman and Patricia O'Brian—*I Know Just What You Mean: The Power of Friendship in Women's Lives.*[1] The authors write that "for grown women, the essence of friendship is talk, telling each other what they're thinking and feeling."[2]

We in Project Renewment talk. We discuss societal influences on the meaning of retirement, our expectations, fears and values. We discuss challenges, decisions, choices and opportunities. We ask why, when, where and how on every topic. And we never have to explain ourselves to each other. We all "get it."

Friendships have always played a major role in women's lives. These special relationships emanate from "childhood, college dorms or a neighborhood of mothers."[3] In some cases, these friendships are sustained; in other cases they diminish over time.

As we age and our lives become more complex, friends become increasingly important. We find ourselves searching for new purposes and passions. On a practical level we look for ways to manage money so we do not outlive our assets. We seek new approaches to maintain our health, and resources and support to provide care for our loved ones. And so often, these needs and challenges occur at the same time. Friends become our source of support, information, understanding and even our safety net.

Because of work demands, many of us have not had the time to develop friendships outside the workplace. One woman put it this way: "My friends have always been my colleagues. After I left my job, I found that I had very little in common with them. I wasn't interested in talking about the company where I had worked. Now at sixty-five, I have to begin to cultivate new friends and I am not sure how to do it."

Making new friends at our life stage can be difficult because many of us are busy with current relationships and commitments. Wall calendars, date books, BlackBerrys and Palm handheld computers remind us that we are overbooked with things to do. We have dates for movies, theater, symphony, grandchildren's recitals, birthday parties and soccer matches, as well as board meetings and other volunteer commitments. We are traveling to the country, to the mountains, to the beach or to the city. We barely have time to keep up with "old" friends.

And yet in Project Renewment, special enduring relationships were spawned. "I established friendships at an early age as my children were growing up. I haven't made such deep friendships in the past thirty-five years—until now."

Our friends are important when we are facing a crisis, and particularly a health crisis. Cancer, a hip replacement, the illness of an adult child and accidents have rallied the women of Project Renewment. Here is an e-mail from one of our women: "Dearest ones: The neck brace was removed today after two months. I feel like a free woman. Thanks for all of your love and caring. It has been my anchor. Millions of hugs to you."

Friends outside Project Renewment were also treasured. "I couldn't have made it through my illness without my friends. I needed them to tell me that I would get better. From this experience I learned which friends I could count on to comfort me. I learned that even those who were very close friends while I was well were not the people I wanted to be with when I was ill. Some friends who were strong and dynamic were exhausting while I was sick."

Women are good listeners and give honest feedback, empathize, understand and care. "I can't talk to my husband about a problem I am having. Before I even get halfway through what I want to say, he begins to problem-solve. He wants to find a solution. I just want a sounding board and only my women friends can provide that."

Men and women differ in their experience of friendships. Men tend to "do" things together while women tend to "be" together.[4] During the old hunter and gathering days, men were the hunters. They stood side by side and didn't speak for fear of scaring off their prey. Women gathered food in the jungle and talked to each other. Rob Becker in his hit comedy *Defending the Caveman* writes, "If a woman (went) for very long without hearing the voice of another woman, she [knew she had] been eaten by an animal."[5]

Research has indicated that women have a special gift that encourages them to relate to other women under stressful conditions. A study conducted by the University of California in Los Angeles suggests that friendships between women diminish the stress in their lives.[6] In addition to the well-known stress response of fight or flight, women have another response, one that counteracts the "kind of stomach-quivering stress most of us experience on a daily basis."[7] They release the hormone oxytocin, which has a calming effect, acting as a buffer to the fight-or-flight response.[8] Consequently, women friendships can soothe us in troubled times.

The Nurses' Health Study from Harvard Medical School reinforces the significance of friendships.[9] With more friends, women are likely to suffer less physical impairments in later life and more likely to be happy with their lives. Results were so significant that the researchers determined that not having friends was as detrimental to one's health as obesity or smoking.

In looking for role models, one of the women spoke about her mother. "My mother is ninety-one years old and in relatively good health. She was widowed at the age of sixty-seven. All of the friends she had at that stage of her life are now deceased. She lives alone, volunteers four days a week at a health care center for older people and plays bridge every Saturday afternoon followed by dinner out. Sundays are a day to spend time with siblings, children and grandchildren and sometimes a movie. At ninety-one the majority of her friends tend to be younger. She is quite happy."

We learn from this woman that there are ways to compensate for losses in older age. As we age, our friends also will become older and some will die before we do. We will miss them and at the same time we must be open to fill the void. This ninety-one-year-old woman stays connected to family and friends on a full-time basis. Just engaging in activities we love provides a fertile environment for developing friendships.

In the 1967 Beatles' album, *Sergeant Peppers Lonely Hearts Club Band*, John Lennon and Paul McCartney recorded "With a Little Help from My Friends." Their line, "I'll get by with a little help from my friends" reminds us we will do just that and more.

Questions to ask yourself:

1. If you have friends at work, what will become of your friendships once you retire?
2. Make a list of your three closest friends. Which ones will be there for you should you decide to retire?
3. What do you expect from a friendship and what are you willing to contribute?
4. What kind of time and energy do you believe is required to develop new friendships at this life stage?
5. How do you meet new friends?

37

A SORORITY HOUSE,
NOT A NURSING HOME

In a hospital they throw you out into the street before you are half cured, but in a nursing home they don't let you out till you are dead.

—GEORGE BERNARD SHAW

Our women thought about life in their older age: "There's a good chance that each of us will be alone. Let's think about pooling our money and buying a big one-story house. We can hire a concierge to manage our services. Instead of a driver, we'll have a chauffeur; instead of a cook, we'll have a chef. We'll have sherry at 4:00 P.M. and weekly chamber music. Aides will assist us as needed and handypersons will install grab bars and change lightbulbs. And we will help each other. Some of us like to sew, others like to bake. We'll have wireless high-speed Internet and the basic communication gadgets of the day. The library will be a combination of all our books. We'll pool our CDs and DVDs. An architect can build a few bungalows in the back for visits from our children and grandchildren. Oh yes, we will have a business manager who will negotiate rates for needed services." Project Renewment women are enjoying thinking about living together.

Having just the right physical environment, services and enriching activities are ideal. However, that's only part of the story. "The most important thing to me would be the companionship and support of friends that come with communal living."

The desire for women to live together is not a surprise. We are part of a generation of women who shared bedrooms with siblings, had pajama parties in high school, joined sororities in college and some of us even lived in communes in our young-adult years. In our early married years, some of us bought groceries through a food co-op. Getting up at 5:00 A.M. we drove to the farmer's market and purchased fifty pounds of potatoes, twenty-five heads of lettuce, ten pounds of cheese and twenty pounds of tomatoes, and then distributed them to fellow commune members.

A "Renewment Residence" is only an idea and somewhat of a "pie in the sky" concept. It does, however, reflect the desire for alternatives to assisted living and nursing homes. The model is based on midlife and older adults' desire to build an "intentional" community, a term used by professionals in the senior housing field. The idea appeals to those of us who want to live with people we like in an environment that reflects our tastes, preferences and needs.

These types of dreams and visions are becoming a reality. Glacier Circle is a good example. It is the country's first self-planned housing development for older persons, a community that has been conceived and designed by those who live in it.[1] Over a five-year period, the owner-residents bought land together, hired an architect and lobbied for zoning changes. They arranged for the construction of eight town houses grouped around a courtyard with a "common house" consisting of a living room and a large kitchen and dining room for communal dinners.[2] The residents plan to lease an apartment under market value to a nurse, who will provide needed medical services.

Another alternative to traditional assisted-living facilities is the model of aging in place. Those of us who want to continue living in familiar environments may find this appealing. A good example is Beacon Hill Village, an innovative nonprofit organization created by residents of Beacon Hill, Massachusetts. Its residents wanted to grow old in their familiar surroundings and resisted moving into assisted-living facilities. "They were unwilling to be herded by a developer into cookie-cutter senior housing and told what to do and when to do it by social workers half their age."[3] "They didn't want to give up Brahms Requiem at St. Paul's Chapel for a sing-along in the old-folks home or high tea at the Ritz-Carlton for luke-warm decaf in the country kitchen."[4] Beacon Hill Village members pay dues for a variety of services: transportation to and from medical appointments with an advocate, home-delivered meals from favorite restaurants, someone to accompany them to the bank or barber shop and a way to summon help if necessary.

Another alternative to traditional retirement communities are "NORCs,"[5] which are naturally occurring retirement communities for older adults living in a defined geographic area. They consist of apartments or neighborhoods where the residents have grown older together, naturally. They like where they live and do not want to move. Supportive services typically are provided by outside agencies with funding from local philanthropies and, to a lesser extent, the U.S. government.

"I will never go into a nursing home." Not a surprising statement for women who value independence. At sixty-five years or older, we have a 43 percent chance of spending some time in a nursing home.[6] We have all heard horror stories about abuse and neglect, not to mention offensive environmental factors such as odors and poorly lit hallways. In reality there are excellent nursing homes, but nagging images and the threat of losing our autonomy throw fear into our hearts.

We are counting on innovators like Dr. William Thomas, a geriatrician and crusader determined to revolutionize nursing home care. He is the originator of the Eden Alternative, a concept and plan to convert nursing home environments to habitats for human beings rather than facilities for the frail and elderly. His alternative is to create vigorous and vibrant housing filled with plants, outdoor gardens, birds, children, care and, most of all, companionship.[7]

In 1991 Thomas transformed his first nursing home. It had more than eighty parakeets, ten finches, two lovebirds, a half-dozen cockatiels and two canaries. Residents and staff adopted all the parakeets and gave each a name. He replaced lawns of the nursing home with gardens of flowers and vegetables, believing that we all have a stake in tilling the soil. The culture of domestic animals and edible plants is possibly the oldest, most common denominator that connects one person to another.[8] Dr. Thomas evaluated his experiment and found that compared to traditional facilities, his residents needed significantly fewer drugs, lived longer and staff turnover was less.

The ideal "Renewment Residence" would resemble another model developed by Thomas, the Green House, a small intentional community for a group of older adults and staff. It is a "place that focuses on life and its heart is found in the relationships that flourish there."[9]

We are a generation of women who are creative and capable of taking our talents and drive to create new ways to live. We may move together into an existing community or we may form our own. One day independent Renewment "Sororities" will be a reality.

Questions to ask yourself:

1. What kind of housing are you in at present?
2. How will your current housing situation work for you as you age?
3. What kinds of changes in your living situation are you planning to make?
4. How do you feel about communal living? How do you feel about living with a friend or relative?
5. What is your ideal living arrangement in your old age?

38

AUTHENTICITY

The authentic self is the soul made visible.

—Sara Ban Breathneck

It is only fitting that the last essay of our book is on authenticity. Understanding our own uniqueness is an essential part of the wisdom we acquire as we get older. It helps us navigate in a complicated world. By facing our own truths, we are better equipped to act on our behalf and on behalf of others.

An executive director of a nonprofit organization spoke about her growing sense of self. "While working, I had to be mindful of all the people around me. At times it was difficult for me to feel authentic. I would not have wanted to risk alienating my staff, board of directors or donors. There were events I attended and social engagements I acccpted because I needed to do that for the advancement of my organization. On many occasions, I allowed the expectations of the outside world to dictate my behavior. And I am okay with that, but now that I am retired I no longer have to make those compromises. The older I get, the better I know myself; and the better I know myself the more authentic I become."

Pema Chodron, through her practice of Buddhism, tells us that "finding our own true nature and speaking from that (and) acting from that" is what we need to do.[1]

"Whatever our quality is, that's our wealth and our beauty; that's what other people respond to."[2]

Our true nature provides the groundwork for an authentic life that is consciously lived. According to existentialists, consciousness and authenticity are closely related. "The conscious self is seen as coming to terms with being in a material world and with encountering external forces, pressures and influences which are very different (from us). . . . Authenticity is the degree to which one is true to one's own personality, spirit, or character despite these pressures."[3]

"My family was horrified when I decided to retire and downsize," said a fifty-five-year-old attorney. "My parents took tremendous pride in my accomplishments. I, on the other hand, felt as if I were disappearing in the maze of the law. In order to make it financially I sold my home and scaled down to an apartment near the beach. Downsizing was difficult and I know I will have to have income beyond my retirement package, but it won't be practicing law. I feel free for the first time in years."

A seventy-year-old retired advertising executive spoke about her life decisions. "I made the choice not to marry, which put me out of step with the rest of the world. Since I am an only child, my parents were disappointed that they never had the opportunity to become grandparents. Every time I got into a relationship, I felt smothered. While I have had my share of lovers, it would be nice to have a lifelong companion now. However, I know myself well enough to know I could not make the concessions required to be in a long-term relationship."

These women came to terms with their authentic selves, not in youth or midlife, but in later life. For some, this time is seen as a relief—a time to finally emerge with confidence and become who they really are.

The women's movement played a profound role in challenging many of us to become introspective. We joined consciousness-raising groups to understand how much of our lives were a product of outside expectations and pressures, and how our authentic selves fit into the picture. Some of us left our marriages, others returned to school and others entered the workplace. We took the first steps in getting acquainted with ourselves and acted upon this new awareness.

The conflict of the conscious self with the pressures from the outside world is a common theme of philosophy, literature, stage and screen. In Henrik Ibsen's A Doll House Nora leaves her cloistered life to find herself. The protagonist in the film The Devil Wears Prada departs the world of high fashion in order to reconnect to her authentic self and her lover.

Arthur Miller's Pulitzer Prize–winning play Death of a Salesman tells the story of the destructiveness of the American dream on the lives of Willy Lohman and his son Happy. We feel hope for Willy's son Biff, who rejects his father's world and moves West to follow his own dreams. Like other playwrights and authors, Arthur Miller pushes us to see the truth in people's lives.

In our quest to find meaning in our lives we must first discover who we are. We have to know our own truths in order to be able to find the core of our identity. This will be different for each of us. Socrates' message that an "unexamined life is not worth living"[4] becomes poignantly relevant as we march through the life stages. It enables us to face the future with clarity, truth and meaning.

It's been quite a ride, and we have not yet reached our destination.

Questions to ask yourself:

1. How well do you know yourself?
2. What are your "truths"?
3. Who are the people who most influence your decisions?
4. Which of your values most influences your thinking and behavior?
5. How authentic a life do you lead?

Part 2

A Guide to Creating a
Project Renewment Group

A Guide to Creating a
Project Renewment Group

▣ ▣ ▣

This guide is designed to assist you in creating and sustaining a Project Renewment group. The guidelines have been tested and effectively used by seven groups of career women in Southern California. Since individual groups are unique in their composition and collective personalities, we recommend modifying and adapting the guidelines as needed.

ABOUT THE GROUP

A Project Renewment group consists of women who focus on their current life stage and the period of time traditionally known as the "retirement years." By sharing their intellect, vision, experience and emotions, women are stimulated to think in new ways about themselves as they contribute to the thinking of other women. Each woman has the opportunity to apply her current and newly acquired knowledge, awareness and insights to her own future.

The groups are not therapy or support sessions. While supportive, Project Renewment groups focus on self-discovery; they build on strengths rather than fixing or repairing.

GETTING STARTED

The impetus for starting a Project Renewment group often comes from just one person. It may be you. Perhaps you have been thinking about retirement and wondering what will happen in the next part of your life. Or perhaps you have been retired a short time and find yourself asking "Is this all there is?" If you are interested in exchanging your thoughts with other women in similar positions or situations, consider launching a Project Renewment group.

FINDING POTENTIAL MEMBERS

It may take several months of talking to friends, friends of friends or people you hardly know about your idea of starting a group. To recruit members, consider organizations you know well and are a member of such as religious, business, professional, philanthropic or recreational groups. Potential members also may come from women in your personal life. Often an interested woman might know several like-minded women. Your group members may have diverse professional backgrounds yet share common values and concerns that are helpful in establishing group cohesiveness.

SELECTING MEMBERS

A successful group is made up of women who know what to expect from their involvement. This can be accomplished by a process that is similar to an interview/orientation. There are no educational or personal requirements for joining. Look for women who have identified with their careers and are in transition or anticipating a transition from their primary career. For those whom you do not know, your first contact may be by phone, e-mail or at a social gathering. It is during this first conversation that it is useful to articulate the purpose of Project Renewment. Discuss your own interests and why you are motivated to form a group. This first informal contact with a potential member typically provides enough information to determine whether or not you should schedule an interview/orientation meeting with that person and other interested women to form a new group.

Ideally, we are able to conduct our first screening of a potential member by phone or in a one-to-one exchange. At this time it is possible for you and the women who are applying to determine if Project Renewment is right for them. Even with this early interaction there will be some women who reach the interview stage who are not a good fit for a group.

This creates a situation that calls on the interviewer's best skills. It is helpful to know about other community resources that may be appropriate for these women. This knowledge enables us to redirect rather than reject.

One woman who applied had been retired for twenty years and was interested in making new friends and engaging in new activities. She was told that the focus of our discussions was on transitions, early stages of retirement and personal growth. She was referred to a local group that met her specific priorities.

The best outcome is one in which there is a mutual agreement between the interviewer and interviewee that her needs and expectations will not be met by a Project Renewment group.

THE INTERVIEW/ORIENTATION PROCESS

The interview/orientation process gives you your best opportunity to get to know potential members and for them to get to know you.

Once you have identified a group of women you believe would make good group members, schedule appointments. It is best to meet with two to four people at a time to observe group interaction and assess group fit. Women who listen and are respectful of others make good group members. Take at least an hour to meet with each potential group and explore their mutual interests by discussing the challenges of retirement and their expectations from the group.

It is sometimes best to have two people meet with the women so that they can share their observations. Your job will be to ask questions that will stimulate conversation that tell you the most about a person in a short amount of time. A significant part of the meeting is listening.

Begin each interview with your reason for wanting to start a group and a brief description of Project Renewment.* Here are some possible interview questions.

1. Tell me about your career and where you are in your retirement plans.
2. What do you believe are the significant challenges of retirement?
3. What makes you interested in such a group?
4. Have you ever been in any kind of group? Tell us about it.
5. How do you feel about being in a group in which you speak very honestly?
6. What is your availability for a monthly meeting?
7. What do you expect from a group?
8. What contribution do you believe you can make to the group?
9. Are you able to make a commitment to attend monthly meetings?

EXPECTATIONS

Expectations are best expressed during the interview meeting. The following were stated by current Project Renewment women.

"I expect a rich dialogue among bright, vital and dynamic women."

"My expectations are to find out how to deal with a lack of daily structure, how to work out better scheduling of free time, how to cope with less recognition and how to fit in some creativity."

"I expect to join with a group of women who would be willing to delve deeply and meaningfully into what they're experiencing and particularly into how they are going about redesigning their lives."

"It's always refreshing to meet new women and to hear what issues are important to them."

---

*The mission of Project Renewment is to provide a forum for career women fifty-five years or older to use their strategic thinking, creativity and vision to forge new directions for their future that are equally, if not more, satisfying than their previous working years.

CHARACTERISTICS OF GOOD CANDIDATES

✦ Women approximately fifty-five years and older who identify with their careers and are approaching, or are in, a transitional stage in their lives.
✦ Women who have self-esteem and are not self-centered.
✦ Women willing to take risks in exploring their future.
✦ Women who listen, are nonjudgmental and are self-disclosing.
✦ Women who show empathy.
✦ Women who have a positive attitude.
✦ Women who are not needy.
✦ Women who are flexible in their thinking and are able to adapt to the norms of the group.
✦ Women you would like to get to know and spend time with.

WHY WOMEN JOIN: TYPICAL REPONSES

"It's an opportunity to find out what the rest of the world is doing, hearing how others are dealing with this transition, learning from the wisdom and the truth of others."

"I want to develop the more creative side of myself and would like to meet other women who have done that."

"I want to join a Project Renewment group because I am experiencing some difficulty in my transition from work to retirement."

"I need help with change. I'm going down a new road and I don't want to go there alone."

"At a time of switching gears, I believe it is valuable to share with others going through the same experience."

"I tend to feel isolated and miss having people around me who understand what I am going through."

"I want to have new people in my life so that I can be exposed to new ideas and new ways of doing things. I also want to be more focused about my future."

GROUP FORMAT

The ideal number for a group is between eight and twelve. A successful format is monthly meetings that rotate among participants' homes. The size of the home or apartment, geographic location or family responsibilities may preclude some members from hosting meetings.

Most groups meet around the dinner hour with meetings lasting about three hours. Some have potluck dinners; others bring brown bags. Whatever the decision, it is best to keep the food part simple. The dinner hour has been chosen for the meeting time to accommodate women who have daytime commitments. And breaking bread together is always good.

FACILITATOR

Groups work best with a facilitator who can guide the discussion. Ideally, the facilitator has had experience in running groups of any type. When that is not possible, less-experienced women step up to the challenge.

"We didn't have a professional facilitator in our group, so we began by taking turns being the facilitator. Some members did not want to participate in that role and that was okay. It seems to be working for us, even though it was a struggle at first." One member commented that leaderless conversations were too superficial.

The ideal situation is for all group members to take responsibility for the group. In a sense, each woman is an owner and has a role in making the group effective. The following roles for the facilitator also apply to all women in the group.

FACILITATOR RESPONSIBILITIES

✦ Articulate the purpose of Project Renewment.
✦ Guide rather than control the discussion.

- ✦ Ensure meetings start and end at an agreed-upon time.
- ✦ Stress confidentiality, openness, active listening and participation.
- ✦ Ensure that no single person monopolizes the discussion.
- ✦ Give everyone an opportunity to speak.
- ✦ Keep the group focused on the topic.
- ✦ Listen and avoid telling members what they ought to do.
- ✦ Encourage group members to communicate in the first person.
- ✦ Notice if someone is not participating and encourage them to contribute.
- ✦ Discourage storytelling (I know a person who has a cousin who has a friend, etc.).
- ✦ Make sure that one person speaks at a time and discourage side conversations.
- ✦ Participate in the discussion and refrain from being an observer by balancing facilitator-participant roles.

OTHER GROUP MEMBERS' RESPONSIBILITIES

- ✦ Suggest topics for discussion.
- ✦ Troubleshoot if a problem occurs.
- ✦ Determine methods of communication such as e-mails.
- ✦ Distribute information regarding meeting time, place and topic.
- ✦ Maintain a group roster.
- ✦ Establish a process for taking meeting notes, if they are wanted by the group.

The facilitator shares responsibilities with other women in the group. Most important is that the meetings are meaningful and enjoyable.

MEETINGS

The First Meeting

The first meeting is a time for women to get to know one another and understand and appreciate each other's backgrounds. To accomplish this, consider the following items.

+ Ask group members to introduce themselves and to tell why they joined Project Renewment. Spend at least one half hour on this.
+ Discuss the purpose of Project Renewment: Explain there is no right or wrong way to explore the next chapter of our lives. Each group can assume the best way to function by adapting the guidelines as needed.
+ Indicate that discussions at the meetings are confidential. Each person is committed to attending and contributing to the group.
+ Review that the goal of the facilitator is to guide the discussion as reflected by the interests of the group and to keep the discussion focused. The group and facilitator determine how long the facilitator remains in that role.
+ Determine the time and location of the next meeting and the dinner plan.
+ Acknowledge that the host for the evening typically takes responsibility for coordinating the meal and providing e-mail directions to her home.
+ Determine how the group would like to use the mealtime. It can be used to socialize or to continue the more focused discussion.

Decisions to make:

+ Where and when to meet
+ Frequency of meetings
+ Which day of the week works best
+ Start and ending time of the meetings

+ Method of communication
+ Who will take meeting notes
+ Who will maintain the group roster that includes contact infor-
mation and a brief description of each woman's career history
+ Who will be the facilitator and whether or not it is one person or
a revolving position
+ Topics for discussion. See page 197 for a recommended list.
The preliminary topic selection can occur at the first meeting
and also at each subsequent meeting.

Like any other group, and particularly one in which women will be
sharing their thoughts, experiences, dreams and feelings, time is
needed to develop trust in one another. Consequently, in the first few
meetings the women will just be getting to know one another. Some
groups will take a few meetings to become cohesive while others may
take longer.

A brief questionnaire used at the start of your group will give you a
profile of the women in your group. See Appendix D. Ask participants
to complete the form at your first meeting.

The Second Meeting

Begin by reviewing procedures established in your first meeting. Make
changes and/or proceed to having the members do a "check-in" with
each other.

A "check-in" is one of the mainstays of the groups. Members report
to each other what has taken place in their lives in the past month.
What is shared is usually relevant to how members explore the experiences and changes taking place in their lives.

Most groups begin with a check-in. Others may do a check-in via
e-mail prior to the meeting or during dinner. Another approach is to
check in only when there is something important to share. Most
women want to know what is happening in their fellow members' lives.
There may be a struggle in deciding how much time should be spent
on members checking in and how much time is spent discussing a
topic. Remember that the focus is the discussion topic.

In the second meeting and into the first year of any group the check-in process is one of the best ways for women to get to know each other.

Following the check-in the members can identify topics they would like to discuss. These may be brought up during the check-in time. Topics can be changed at the last minute to more relevant subjects. The end of the session is a good time to select a topic for the next meeting.

Future Meetings

Subsequent meetings will follow the process established by the group. Changes may occur as members get to know each other better and discover the best procedures for them. Keep in mind that women want to feel that the time they spend in Project Renewment is worthwhile. The immediate goal is for them to leave knowing that they learned something new, acquired a new insight or were inspired by other women . . . and had a great time doing it.

One Year Later

After one year, it is helpful to get a sense of the group, their priorities and expectations. See Appendix E for a survey. This can be distributed at a meeting or by e-mail.

BEST PRACTICES

A Seven-Year Summary

The following guidelines summarize the best practices accumulated over a seven-year period of meetings.

+ All group discussions are strictly confidential. Participants must be assured that nothing they say will be repeated. These groups provide a safe place for women to be who they are, not a place where they must maintain their public persona.
+ The issues being discussed belong to the individual Project Renewment group. The purpose of the groups is to assist women

through a life stage that for many can be challenging and difficult. Above all, this is not a commercial venture that can be capitalized upon by others.

✦ Participants make a commitment to attend all meetings unless they are traveling or have an unavoidable conflict. Unless there is an emergency, the hostess needs adequate notice if a member plans to miss a meeting.

✦ All members of the group are expected to participate. No one who attends is expected to be an observer, which includes the facilitator.

✦ Groups meet on a monthly basis. An effort is made to accommodate participants' schedules. Meetings usually occur on a specified weekday in the evening. Members share a potluck dinner and meetings are held in participants' homes on a rotating basis. The meeting host determines the menu and organizes the meal. Women who have special diets that cannot be accommodated at a regular meal may want to bring their own food.

✦ A private meeting space is provided since discussions are confidential.

✦ Group members have responsibilities. These include maintaining a group roster, keeping the group discussion focused, selecting topics, gathering information for specific issues, maintaining a "one person at a time" talking policy, giving everyone an opportunity to speak, limiting soliloquies and preventing others from interrupting. Each group can decide how these tasks will be handled.

✦ Meetings begin with a check-in, at which time members can report on issues that they discussed at the previous meeting and/or new issues in their lives that are relevant to transition and change.

✦ Participants speak in the first person. It is more effective to share personal experiences, opinions and insights than to give advice. For example, rather than say "What you ought to do is," one can say "What I have tried in that situation, or what worked for me in that kind of situation . . ." Although we do not analyze each other, we are free to suggest why we believe we are behaving in a way that might not be in our best interests.

✦ Cell phones are turned off. In general, telephone calls should not be answered unless there is an emergency. In that case, inform the group ahead of the discussion that there might be an interruption.

✦ A date for the next meeting is determined.

✦ E-mail is used as the most efficient way to communicate. For anyone who is not computer literate it is suggested she learn about e-mail and attachments and/or find a member of the group who is willing to provide her with materials and information. E-mail should be checked regularly to stay informed.

✦ One group member writes a brief summary of the major issues discussed and sends it by e-mail to the other women in the group. Keeping such a summary gives the group a sense of achievement, history and reference points. The group facilitator maintains the reports for future reference and use.

✦ Aggravating behavior is discouraged. If a behavior or attitude by someone is particularly detrimental to the group, find a way as quickly as you can to sensitively address and solve the problem.

✦ Project Renewment does not evolve into psychotherapy. However, members are encouraged to share crises that occur as part of life and are likely to have an impact on everyone. These life events tend to increase with age. The success of the group will depend on allowing this kind of sharing without becoming involved with a process of therapy.

✦ Add to and modify this list of best practices and enjoy your involvement.

WHY GROUPS WORK

Groups work well for many reasons. Yet so much depends on the chemistry of the members. Existing group members have identified the following characteristics as key to a successful group:

✦ Authenticity: being true to ourselves, saying what we think, believe and feel about issues.
✦ Communication: speaking, listening, understanding, processing and responding with clarity.
✦ Ownership: each member is the owner of the group and takes responsibility for making the group work. Group success is a priority, even though each person attends as an individual.
✦ Honesty: honesty does not only operate on a feeling level, but also on an intellectual level. This honesty moves the group to greater sensitivity, awareness, creativity and provocative thinking.
✦ Respect: each member of the group is entitled to her own point of view. Disagreements make discussions even better. A genuine respect for what others experience, think, believe or envision makes the gathering different from usual day-to-day activities.

WHY GROUPS DON'T WORK

It is not unusual for a group to go through various stages of adjustment. Here are some of the most common reasons for difficulties in a group:

✦ One person dominates the discussion.
✦ The members are not committed. When members are absent it causes the group dynamics to change and discussions lose depth and richness.
✦ The discussion becomes superficial.

Here are some essential dos and don'ts.
✦ Do schedule meetings at a designated time of the month.

- ✦ Do start and end on time.
- ✦ Keep initial check-ins brief—about three minutes per person. However, if someone is going through unusual times, exceptions are appropriate.
- ✦ Don't story-tell about other people. Always speak in the first person.
- ✦ Don't have cross-talk or have side conversations.
- ✦ Don't give examples irrelevant to the topic.
- ✦ Don't forget to plan the topics for the next meeting.

A WRONG FIT

The attrition rate for the existing Project Renewment groups has been low. Even with the best interviewing process, some women will leave the group because of life events, a move to a new city or because their expectations are not met. If a woman's only interest is in finding new friends rather than experiencing growth, it is reasonable for that woman to withdraw.

SECONDARY GAINS

Project Renewment has yielded unintentional and wonderful consequences. Establishing new friendships and finding new resources for daily living are just a few benefits from group membership. Women also have found others to join them for favorite activities such as hiking, walking and cultural activities. Two yearly educational and social events provide the opportunity for women to meet others outside their group. Each event continues to expand and enrich the women's involvement.

DISCUSSION TOPICS AND QUESTIONS

The thirty-eight essays in this book are potential topics for Project Renewment discussions. Occasionally, a subject(s) that surfaces during the check-in will be transformed into a topic for the current meeting.

The following topics and sets of questions have been successfully used by current Project Renewment groups.

Productivity

+ How have you defined being "productive" throughout your life?
+ In which ways does this definition work or not work for you today?
+ What are the turning points in your life that have influenced your current definition of being productive?

Passion

+ How has feeling passionate about your work influenced your life and career?
+ What role does passion play in your life today?
+ How do you see the pursuit of passion in your life today and into the future?

Recognition/Validation

+ How has validation and recognition affected your past decisions and the ways in which you worked and have lived your life?
+ How does your need for recognition and validation continue to influence the way in which you live your life today?
+ What makes you feel recognized and validated today?

Values

+ What are the core values that have best served you throughout your life and career?
+ Which of these values continues to work for you and which, if any, have become barriers to the way in which you want to live your life today?
+ What value do you place on being able to earn money?

Money, Money, Money

+ What do you need to have financially to feel safe and comfortable in your retirement?
+ How much do you know about your finances?
+ How have you been influenced by societal attitudes about money?
+ How do you feel about working during retirement?

Creativity

+ How would you describe the ways in which you have expressed your creativity in your life and work?
+ In which ways would you like to continue to express and/or newly discover your creativity as you move into the future?
+ What are your everyday activities that make you feel creative?

Travel

+ How much and what kind of travel do you want to undertake?
+ How do you find the right kinds of trips and travel companions?
+ What kind of conditions do you need in the places to which you travel?
+ What part of your income are you willing to dedicate to travel?

Relationships

+ How would you describe your relationships with family, friends and colleagues?
+ How much contact with people do you need?
+ What changes, if any, would you like to make in your most significant relationships?
+ How could you develop new friendships?

Success

+ What replaces the career-related feelings of success and importance?

+ How do you define success?
+ How do the people around you describe success?
+ Where else in your life do you feel successful?

Spirituality

+ How do you define spirituality or an inner life for yourself?
+ How can you build a more spiritual life?
+ How have spiritual practices impacted your life and career?
+ Who can be your spiritual mentor?
+ In which ways will spirituality influence your life today and into the future?

Giving Back/Volunteering

+ How has giving back to the community been a part of your life?
+ Have you reached the point in your life where you believe you have given enough or are you ready to give more?
+ What causes are important to you?
+ What would interest you enough to inspire you to work without pay?
+ How can you find volunteer activities that might interest you?

Health

+ What are the lifestyle activities you follow in order to maintain your health and well-being?
+ How do you see maintaining or changing these activities as you move into the future?
+ How does public policy impact your health?
+ Who are the participants in your health care?
+ How could you find a gym that would be good for you?
+ How could you put together a walking group?

Home

+ How much time do you like to spend at home?
+ What is your need for space and privacy?

- How do you convey your need for space and privacy to a spouse or partner?
- How can you make your home more comfortable and safe?

Maintaining Independent Living

- What do you believe you will have to do for yourself in order to live an independent life into your old age?
- How do you feel about the things and people on whom you feel dependent?
- What kind of housing will you need in your later years?

Stimulation

- How much intellectual and social stimulation do you need in your life?
- What will replace the stimulation you have had in your work?
- What things/experiences are stimulating to you?

Loss/Gains

- How would you describe the losses and gains associated with your retirement?
- How would you describe the losses and gains associated with aging?
- How does the inevitability and proximity of death impact how you are living today?

Vulnerability

- What are the areas in your life that make you feel the most vulnerable?
- How do you feel about being vulnerable?
- With whom can you be vulnerable?

Power

- What makes you feel powerful?
- When do you experience a loss of power?
- How much power do you need or want?

Friendships

✦ How do you feel about your current friendships?
✦ What do they mean to you?
✦ What would you look for in new friendships?
✦ Where might you look for them?

Legacy

✦ What would you like your legacy to be?
✦ Who has influenced your perception of a legacy?
✦ What are you doing to make your legacy a reality?

Wisdom

✦ How do you define wisdom?
✦ How do you recognize your own wisdom?
✦ In what situations or circumstances do you feel the most or least wise?

Change

✦ How do you feel about change?
✦ When is change okay or not okay?
✦ What changes in your life were particularly painful and why?
✦ What in your life would you like to change?

Lifelong Learning

✦ How interested are you in pursuing educational courses?
✦ What subjects pique your curiosity?
✦ How do you find out about educational opportunities?

Husbands/Partners

✦ How does your retirement affect your husband or partner?
✦ Are you planning to retire at the same time? If not, how will this affect your life?
✦ What kind of changes, if any, will be necessary in your relationship once you are retired?

+ How much time would you like to spend together? Apart?
+ How will you share household chores?

Sex

+ What changes, if any, would you like to make in your sex life?
+ What do sex and sexuality mean to you?
+ What role does sex play in your relationships?
+ How would you describe your own sexuality?

Aging

+ What do you see when you look in the mirror?
+ How do you feel about growing older?
+ What messages do you get from the antiaging industry?

Energy

+ How do you feel about your energy level?
+ What diminishes your energy?
+ What can you do to improve your energy level?

Caregiving

+ What kind of caregiving responsibilities do you have?
+ What kind of caregiving responsibilities do you foresee in the future?
+ How do you feel about your caregiving role?
+ How much time do you want to spend in caregiving activities with parents, spouses, children, grandchildren or friends?
+ Have you explored all possible ways of getting help?
+ How much time do you put aside for yourself?

Taking Risks

+ How do you feel about trying new activities even though you might have been discouraged from doing them in the past?
+ What kinds of risks do/did you take in the workplace? In your personal life?

- ✦ What have you always wanted to do?
- ✦ What stands in your way of trying new things?

Death and Dying

- ✦ How does the inevitability of death impact your life today?
- ✦ What preparations have you made for your death?
- ✦ How do you respond to the death of family and friends?

GOOD TO GO . . .

These guidelines are based on eight years of witnessing the positive impact of Project Renewment on women's lives. We know the process can be duplicated. The enduring communities of career women have opened our eyes to the rich possibilities of this time of our lives.

The secondary gains from Project Renewment are also valuable. New friendships and connections to other women sharing life stage challenges and social and recreational activities are common occurrences. And taking life risks together makes the risks seem smaller.

We hope you will start a group. And please stay in touch with us through our website www.ProjectRenewment.com and let us know how you are doing. Our best wishes to each of you for a fabulous journey, extraordinary destination and infinite health, joy and fulfillment.

Appendixes

Appendix A

⊡ ⊡ ⊡

ACKNOWLEDGMENTS

The voices, wisdom and stories of Project Renewment women fill these pages. We are forever grateful for their generosity in sharing their thoughts, experiences, vision, spirit and feelings. All of the personal stories come from them. Some professions connected to the stories have been changed for purposes of confidentiality.

We thank our founding members, Lillian Frank, Barbara Goldberg, Barbara Hammer, Sherry May, Audrey Stein and Lois Zells, who worked with us to pioneer the concept and direction of Project Renewment. They encouraged us to write a book about our years together talking around the table. We value the contributions of Myrna Hant and Marlene Gilbert to the early development of the Project Renewment guide.

A special appreciation and thank-you is extended to Dr. Sherry May, Dr. Edward Kaufman and Lois Zells for their tireless reading and recommendations. We appreciate the advice from Kathy and Mark Bloomfield, who were the first to tell us that Project Renewment was a concept and model to be shared in a book. Our gratitude is extended to journalist Elizabeth Pope, who introduced us to the public and in doing so connected us to Scribner. And a special thank-you to literary agent Pat Karlan for her guidance in the early phases of the project.

Our team was superb. We thank Kathryn Thomas for her dedication and her expert research, editorial and administrative assistance, and Lahni Baruck, our illustrator, whose talent, creativity, understanding and patience translated our vision into illustrations. We would also like to thank Echo Chang for her research on midlife women.

207

A very special appreciation is extended to Beth Wareham, our superb editor at Scribner; Carolyn Reidy, president and CEO of Simon & Schuster; and Susan Moldow, publisher of Scribner, who believed in this book and gave us the opportunity to highlight Renewment as the centerpiece of retirement.

Appendix B

□ □ □

WOMEN OF PROJECT RENEWMENT (1999–2007)— PARTIAL LISTING

Maria Appleman
Lois Bader
Harriet Bay
Judith Benson
Bernice Bratter
Louise Caplan
Kathy Cucher
Linda Damon
Tama Deitch
Helen Dennis
Judith Farber
Lillian Frank
Marlene Gilbert
Jane Glenn Haas
Barbara Goldberg
Virginia Greco
Joelle Green
Lee Gale Gruen
Barbara Hammer
Myrna Hant
Ida Beal Harding
Helen Hasenfeld
Shelia Hutman
Sally James
Marilyn Jellison
Joanne Jubelier
Judith Karasik
Nancy Kirshberg
Stella Krieger
Elizabeth Lawrence

Jo Ann Lesser
Toni Martinez-Burgoyne
Alice March
Sherry May
Beth Meltzer
Sue Miller
Betsy Morgan
Arlene Newman
Joy Nuell
Judith Palarz
Audrey Parker
Berta Pitt
Mary Rapoport
Helen Reid
Linda Rose
Julie Roth
Suzanne Ryan
Linda Scheck
Frances Schwartz
Marcia Seligson
Bonnie Stark
Audrey Stein
Jane Alexander Stewart
Adrienne Stokols
Sally Sussman
Janice Tarr
Priscilla Ulene
Margot Winchester
Joyce Zaitlan
Lois Zells

Appendix C

⊡ ⊡ ⊡

SURVEY DATA FROM PROJECT RENEWMENT GROUPS

- More than one-third of the Renewment women do volunteer or pro bono work in the community on a regular basis. Eight percent of the women contribute more than 10 hours per week and 16 percent volunteer less than 10 hours per week.
- Flexibility is important to women in this life stage. More than 75 percent of the women are interested in occasional volunteer opportunities, compared to just 40 percent who are interested in regularly scheduled volunteer opportunities.
- The most significant concerns of Project Renewment women at this point in their lives are adapting to changing health, replacing work with something meaningful, achieving/maintaining financial security, feeling a sense of achievement and allowing themselves to have fun and experience more enjoyment.
- At this life stage, the top activity priorities of Renewment women include improving or staying fit, cultural/intellectual/creative pursuits, travel, family and friends.
- Seventy-one percent of Project Renewment women rated their overall life satisfaction as "very satisfied" and 21 percent said they were "somewhat satisfied." Only one woman expressed dissatisfaction with life.
- Thirty-eight percent of the women consider themselves "retired."

Appendix D

🔳 🔳 🔳

NEW MEMBER SURVEY

1. Name: _____

2. Date of Birth: _____

3. Address:_____

4. Phone: _____

5. E-mail: _____

6. My primary career is or was:

_____

_____

7. I consider myself:
___retired ___employed ___ partly retired

___ partly employed ___other

8. I was motivated to join the group because

_____

_____

_____

9. The two most important topics for me are

_____

_____

Appendix E

⊞ ⊞ ⊞

FOLLOW-UP SURVEY

1. Age: _____   Today's date _____

2. Date of Birth: _____

3. Marital Status:

___ Married
___ Single/Divorced
___ Single/Widowed
___ Other
___ Single/Never Married

Work Status: (You may check more than one category.)

___ Retired
___ Work Full-Time (for others)
___ Work Full-Time (self-employed)
___ Work Part-Time (for others)
___ Work Part-Time (self-employed)
___ Pro bono/Volunteer/Civic engagement work (more than
       ten hours a week)
___ Pro bono/Volunteer/Civic engagement work (less than
       ten hours a week)
___ (Other) Please specify _____

4. What was your last (or current) profession?

_____

5. How do (or did) you feel about your most recent work/job?
(You can check more than one.)

____ Love (loved) it
____ Enjoy (enjoyed) it
____ Ambivalent about it
____ Will be (was) thrilled to leave it

6. What do you think is the most meaningful benefit of Project Renewment?

_____

_____

_____

_____

7. Please put 1, 2 and 3 next to your **3 most significant concerns** at this point in your life. (1 = most significant concern)

____ Adapting to changing health
____ Coping with boredom
____ Changing family relationships
____ Financial security
____ Feeling a sense of achievement
____ Having fun; experiencing more enjoyment
____ Lack of structure in my life
____ Lack of intellectual stimulation
____ Support for aging family members
____ Making new friends; expanding my social contacts
____ Replacing work with something meaningful
____ Doing things I've never done before
____ Making a contribution on behalf of others (other than family)
____ Other. Please specify _____

8. Please put 1, 2 and 3 next to your **3 top activity priorities** at this point in your life. (1 = top priority)

____ Cultural/intellectual events—theater, museums, concerts, etc.
____ Finding new work alternatives
____ Volunteer work/community service/philanthropy
____ Travel
____ Improving computer/Internet skills
____ Financial planning/investments

___ Improving your health or staying fit (exercise/sports /spas, retreats/health programs)

___ Taking classes, pursuing a new area of study

___ Creative pursuits (crafts, painting, drawing, photography, music, creative writing, etc.)

___ Spiritual/religious pursuits

___ Caring for a husband/partner

___ Caring/being with grandchildren

___ Other interests or ideas; please specify

_____

_____

9. Put a check mark next to the phrase that applies to your feelings about financial security:

___ I am very concerned about my financial security

___ I am moderately concerned about my financial security

___ Financial security is not an issue for me

10. Would you be interested in paid employment?
    ___ Yes ___ No ___ Maybe

    If "maybe," what are your considerations?

_____

_____

_____

11. Would you be interested in regularly scheduled volunteer opportunities?

___ Yes ___ No

12. Would you be interested in volunteering on an occasional basis?

___Yes ___ No

13. In the last year, has your health impacted your ability to work and/or participate in other activities you enjoy?

___ Yes ___ No

If yes, how?

_____

_____

_____

14. Which statement best describes your overall satisfaction with your life?

____ Very satisfied
____ Somewhat satisfied
____ Not very satisfied
____ Not at all satisfied

15. What are some of the things that might enhance your life?

_____

_____

_____

16. At this point in your life, what brings you the greatest joy?

_____

_____

_____

_____

17. Comments:

_____

_____

_____

_____

_____

_____

18. Your name:

_____

Appendix F

⊡ ⊡ ⊡

WEBSITES

CAREGIVING

- http://www.aarp.org/families/caregiving_help
  Resources for caregivers from AARP.

- http://www.caregiving.org
  National Alliance for Caregiving is a nonprofit coalition that provides support to family caregivers and increases public awareness of family caregiving issues.

- http://www.aoa.gov/prof/aoaprog/caregiver/caregiver.asp
  Resource room for caregivers, families and professionals from the U.S. Administration on Aging's National Family Caregiver Support Program.

- www.caregiver.org
  Family Caregiver Alliance
  The Family Caregiver Alliance, through their education, services, research and advocacy, is the public voice for caregivers.

- http://www.caps4caregivers.org
  Children of Aging Parents
  A national nonprofit organization that provides reliable information, referrals and support to family caregivers and works to heighten public awareness about the importance of caregiver health.

- http://www.eldercare.gov
  Eldercare Locator
  (800) 677-1116

Sponsored by the U.S. Administration on Aging, Eldercare Locator is a public service that provides information about state and local agencies and community-based organizations that serve older adults and caregivers.

CASKETS AND PLOTS

■ http://www.aarp.org/families/grief_loss/a2004-11-15-arrangements.html
Overview information from AARP about funeral arrangements and memorial services.

■ http://www.us-funerals.com/caskets.html
Information from US-Funerals.com about things to consider when buying a casket.

■ http://www.ehow.com/how_3461_buy-cemetery-plot.html
Information from eHow.com about how to buy a cemetery plot.

DEALING WITH ILLNESS

■ http://www.merck.com/mmpe/index.html
The Merck Manuals Online Medical Library provides online health information for health professionals and consumers.

■ http://www.pdrhealth.com
PDRhealth, part of Thomson Healthcare, provides disease overviews and information about prescription drugs, clinical trials, and health and wellness.

■ http://www.reutershealth.com/en/index.html
Reuters Health provides medical and healthcare news. The site allows you to customize your news to cover only a specific disease or therapeutic area.

■ http://cancerweb.ncl.ac.uk/omd
A searchable online medical dictionary.

- http://www.webmd.com

  WebMD, an online health resource, includes information about health, wellness, drugs and treatments. Also includes a symptom checker.

DEATH OF A SPOUSE OR LOVED ONE

- http://www.aarp.org/families/grief_loss

  Resources from AARP on the topic of grief and loss.

- http://www.aarp.org/families/grief_loss/a2004-11-15-finaldetails.html

  A list from AARP of the basic finance-related actions you will need to take during the first few months following the death of a loved one.

- http://www.aarp.org/families/grief_loss/a2004-11-15-necessary papers.html

  A checklist of documents you will need to gather following the death of a loved one in order to take care of financial matters and file for various benefits.

DEPRESSION/MENTAL HEALTH

- http://www.helpguide.org/index.htm

  A nonprofit resource guide for mental health, healthy lifestyles and aging issues.

- http://www.nlm.nih.gov/medlineplus/depression.html

  Extensive information and resources about depression from the National Institutes of Health and the U.S. National Library of Medicine.

- http://www.niapublications.org/agepages/depression.asp

  Information and resources about depression from the National Institute on Aging.

FINANCES

- http://www.wife.org/relationshipwithmoney.htm
  Article from the Women's Institute for Financial Education (WIFE), which contains questions for you to ask yourself to help you explore your relationship with money.

- http://www.soulofmoney.org/index.php/about/about-the-book/excerpts
  A book excerpt from *The Soul of Money: Transforming Your Relationship with Money and Life.*

- http://iasp.brandeis.edu/womenandaging/finances/giget started.html
  Information about the Wealth Care Kit from the National Endowment for Financial Education. The kit contains worksheets to help you evaluate your current finances, to identify goals and a plan to reach your goals.

- www.wiser.heinz.org
  WISER Women
  A nonprofit organization focused on issues surrounding women's retirement income. WISER provides information and training to women, educators and policy makers.

HOSPICE

National Hospice & Palliative Care Organization

- www.caringinfo.org
  Caring Connections
  (800) 658-8898
  Caring Connections, a program of the National Hospice and Palliative Care Organization (NHPCO), provides free materials about end-of-life issues such as hospice, advance-care planning, grief, financial planning and workplace flexibility.

FITNESS

■ http://www.aarp.org/health/fitness
AARP's physical fitness portal includes tips about sports, exercise, motivation, hydration, etc.

■ http://www.aarp.org/health/fitness/work_out/a2003-04-04-pilates.html
Pilates information from AARP.

■ http://www.aarp.org/health/fitness/work_out/a2003-03-07-yoga.html
Information about the mental and physical benefits of yoga from AARP.

GRANDPARENTING

■ http://www.aarp.org/families/grandparents
Grandparenting resources from AARP.

■ http://www.grandparentsmagazine.net
Information and resources from *Grandparents Magazine*. Site includes city guides, coloring pages, gift ideas, song lyrics, grandparent rights and product reviews.

■ http://www.aarp.org/families/grandparents/raising_grandchild
Supportive resources from AARP for grandparents raising grandchildren.

LIFELONG LEARNING

■ http://www.elderhostel.org
Elderhostel is a not-for-profit organization that provides learning adventures for people fifty-five and over.

■ http://www.roadscholar.org/why/faq.asp
Road Scholar is an educational travel organization for lifelong learners.

■ http://www.usm.maine.edu/olli/national/about.jsp

The national resource center for the Osher Lifelong Learning Institutes includes such features as a network of lifelong learning programs at universities around the country and information about how to find an institute near you.

MEDICARE

■ http://www.medicare.gov

Centers for Medicare & Medicaid Services
7500 Security Boulevard
Baltimore, MD 21244-1850
(800) 772-1213
(800) MEDICARE

The official U.S. government site for information about Medicare; includes information about enrollment, plan choices and billing.

■ http://www.medicare.gov/Library/PDFNavigation/PDF
  Interim.asp?Language=English&Type=Pub&PubID=10050

"Medicare & You 2007"

Answers to the most frequently asked questions about Medicare and a summary of benefits, rights and protections.

■ http://www.medicare.gov/MedicareEligibility/home.asp?
  version=default&browser=Firefox%7C2%7CWinXP&
  language=English

"Medicare Eligibility Tool"

The dynamic Medicare Eligibility Tool asks a series of questions and displays detailed information tailored to your specific situation.

■ http://www.ssa.gov/mediinfo.htm

"Medicare Resources"

Information about replacing a card, coverage, costs, new rules for beneficiaries with high income and more.

MEMORY

- http://www.aarp.org/health/brain
  Brain health resources from AARP including information about how the brain works, how it changes with age and tips for maintaining optimal brain health.

- http://positscience.com
  Posit Science, a San Francisco–based company, has created a scientifically proven brain fitness program.

- http://www.cognifit.com/?page=6
  CogniFit, an Israel-based company, has created research-based techniques and programs to measure, test and train cognitive abilities and psychomotor skills.

- http://www.brainage.com/launch.jsp
  Brain Age is a cognitive fitness game created by Nintendo.

MY SOUL

- http://www.jenniferhawthorne.com/store/chickensoup_women.html
  Information about the *Chicken Soup for the Women's Soul*, a collection of true stories about the spirit of women.

- http://www.jenniferhawthorne.com/store/chickensoup_women2.html
  A *Second Chicken Soup for the Women's Soul* contains 101 additional stories celebrating the experiences of women.

NONPROFIT ORGANIZATIONS FOR MIDLIFE WOMEN IN TRANSITION

- https://www.thetransitionnetwork.org
  The Transition Network
  "A gateway for information, a community of peers, a catalyst for exploring opportunities and a voice for professional women in transition."

■ http://www.womansage.com
Woman Sage
"A mentoring organization dedicated to educating, empowering and fostering relationships among women and midlife."

NOT A TRADITIONAL NURSING HOME

■ http://www.edenalt.com/welcome.htm

Eden Alternative is a nonprofit organization founded by geriatrician William Thomas, who believes aging should be "a continued stage of development and growth, rather than a period of decline." Eden Alternative has been focused on "de-institutionalizing the culture and environment of today's nursing homes and other long-term care institutions."

■ http://www.ncbcapitalimpact.org/default.aspx?id=148

Information about The Green House model, also created by Dr. William Thomas. The Green House model is defined as "a small intentional community for a group of elders and staff. It is a place that focuses on life, and its heart is found in the relationships that flourish there."

■ http://www.aarp.org/families/housing_choices/

Information about housing choices from AARP. Includes information about assisted living facilities, nursing homes and other options.

■ http://www.aarp.org/families/home_design/

Information about home design, safety and universal design from AARP. Includes checklists to help you evaluate the safety and livability of your home.

■ www.alfa.org
Assisted Living Federation of America
ALFA is the largest national association of professionally operated assisted living communities and provides resources to seniors and their families. The website includes a directory of assisted living facilities that are members of ALFA.

PERSONAL PLANNING

- http://www.aarp.prg/families/end_life

  Resources for end-of-life preparation from AARP such as estate planning, powers of attorney and living wills.

- http://www.aarp.org/families/end_life/a2003-12-04-endoflife-guide.html

  An estate planning guide from AARP.

- http://www.help4srs.org/finance/fs-estateplanning.html

  An estate planning fact sheet from H.E.L.P. (Healthcare and Elderlaw Programs), nonprofit information resource for older adults

SEX

- http://www.aarpmagazine.org/lifestyle/relationships/sex_in_america.html

  A summary of the results of AARP's landmark nationwide sex study focused on Americans from midlife to old age.

- http://www.aarpmagazine.org/lifestyle/relationships

  AARP's online guide to relationships.

- http://www.aarpmagazine.org/lifestyle/a2003-09-24-10 smart.html

  "10 Smart First-Date Ideas for Singles 50+" from *AARP The Magazine.*

SOCIAL SECURITY

- http://www.ssa.gov

  (800) 772-1213

  TTY (800) 325-0778

  The official website of the U.S. Social Security Administration, which contains extensive information about retirement benefits, Medicare, disability and Supplemental Security Income (SSI) and other programs.

Social Security Administration
Office of Public Inquiries
Windsor Park Building
6401 Security Blvd.
Baltimore, MD 21235

■ http://www.ssa.gov/howto.htm
"Popular Social Security Services"
Quick links to information about how to access Social Security's most popular services.

■ https://s044a90.ssa.gov/apps6z/FOLO/fo001.jsp
Local Office Locator
Locator tool allows you to search by zip code for information and directions to your local Social Security office and other agencies in your area.

VOLUNTEERING/CIVIC ENGAGEMENT

■ http://www.experiencecorps.org/index.cfm
Homepage for Experience Corps, a nonprofit organization that helps Americans over age fifty-five find meaningful volunteer opportunities.

■ http://www.freedomcorps.gove/about_usafc/initiatives/index.asp
USA Freedom Corps, created in 2002 by President George W. Bush, is a volunteer network for Americans of all ages and backgrounds. The organization focuses on the following three areas of need: "responding in case of crisis at home, rebuilding our communities, and extending American compassion throughout the world."

- http://www.pointsoflight.org
Points of Light Foundation & Volunteer Center National Network
The Points of Light Foundation & Volunteer Center National Network, through its various programs and services, encourages people from all walks of life to volunteer. Their programs include 1-800-Volunteer.org and a 50+ Volunteering Initiative.

- http://www.escus.org/index.html
Executive Service Corps
A nationwide network of volunteer consultants who have had senior level positions in business, government and nonprofits that provide quality, affordable services to nonprofits, schools and government agencies.

- http://www.escus.org/where.html
Executive Service Corps (ESC) Affiliate Network
Directory of local ESC Affiliates.

- www.score.org
SCORE
"Working or retired business owners, executives and corporate leaders who share their wisdom and lessons learned in business" as volunteer counselors to entrepreneurs. Includes information about how to become a volunteer.

- http://www.civicventures.org
Civic Ventures
"Civic Ventures brings together older adults with a passion for service and helps stimulate opportunities for using their talents to advance the greater good."

- www.experiencecorps.org
Experience Corps
A service program for people over fifty-five, Experience Corps members tutor and mentor elementary school students to improve literacy.

WIDOWHOOD

■ http://www.aarp.org/families/grief_loss/a2004-11-15-
newlywidowed.html

A guide for newly widowed titled "On Being Alone," published by AARP, provides a list of eight simple yet important things to remember during this difficult time.

■ http://www.jenniferhawthorne.com/store/chickensoup_
single.html

Reviews and provides information about *Chicken Soup for the Single's Soul,* a book written by singles about "the unique challenges and joys of enjoying life as a single person."

■ http://www.aarp.org/families/grief_loss/a2004-11-15-
claiming.html

Information from AARP about claiming benefits from the Social Security Administration, Veterans Administration and/or a previous employer.

WOMEN AND RETIREMENT

■ http://www.aaup.org/AAUP/pubsres/academe/2004/MJ/
Feat/glaz.html

Article about women and retirement. Article references additional books on the topic.

■ http://www.wiser.heinz.org/portal

Women's Institute for a Secure Retirement (WISER), a non-profit, national resource center, provides various fact sheets, booklets and a quarterly newsletter for women, educators and policy makers.

■ http://www.dol.gove/ebsa/publications/women.html

The Department of Labor Employee Benefits Security Administration provides resources for women. The site contains eight questions to ask yourself and links to booklets such as *Savings Fitness: A Guide to Your Money and Your Financial Future* and *Taking the Mystery Out of Retirement Planning.*

WOMEN TRAVEL/ADVENTURE

- http://www.adventurewomen.com
  AdventureWomen is a travel organization that organizes adventure trips especially for women.

- http://www.tripsforwomen.com
  A travel company which specializes in escorted and non-escorted women's-only trips.

- http://www.travelocity.com/AARP/home/1,5259,AARP /home/EN,00.html?currentPg=home&Service= AARP&subNavPg
  AARP Passport is a travel booking site powered by Travelocity.

Appendix G

⊞ ⊞ ⊞

BOOKS OF INTEREST

Successful Aging by John W. Rowe, M.D., and Robert L. Kahn Ph.D. (New York: Random House, 1998).

The Creative Age: Awakening Human Potential in the Second Half of Life by Gene D. Cohen, M.D., Ph.D. (New York: Harper Collins, 2000).

The Mature Mind: The Positive Power of the Aging Brain by Gene D. Cohen, M.D., Ph.D. (New York: Basic Books, 2005).

AgeLess: Take Control of Your Age and Stay Youthful for Life by Edward L. Schneider, M.D., and Elizabeth Miles (Pennsylvania: Rodale Books, 2003).

The Memory Bible: An Innovative Strategy for Keeping Your Brain Young by Gary Small, M.D. (New York: Hyperion, 2002).

The Memory Prescription: Dr. Gary Small's 14-Day Plan to Keep Your Brain and Body Young by Gary Small, M.D. (New York: Hyperion, 2004).

Encore: Finding Work That Matters in the Second Half of Life by Marc Freedman (New York: PublicAffairs, 2007)

Prime Time: How Baby Boomers Will Revolutionize Retirement and Transform America by Marc Freedman (New York: PublicAffairs, 1999).

My Time: Making the Most of the Rest of Your Life by Abigail Trafford (New York: Basic Books, 2004).

Inventing the Rest of Our Lives: Women in Second Adulthood by Suzanne Braun Levine (New York: Penguin Group, 2005).

Women Confronting Retirement: A Nontraditional Guide edited by Nan Bauer-Maglin and Alice Radosh (New Jersey: Rutgers University Press, 2003).

Leap! What Will We Do with the Rest of Our Lives? by Sara Davidson (New York: Random House, 2007).

Notes

⊡ ⊡ ⊡

INTRODUCTION

1. Bauer-Maglin, Nan, and Radosh, Alice, *Women Confronting Retirement* (New Brunswick: Rutgers University Press, 2003), p. 5.

2. Ibid.

3. Harvard Generations Policy Program, "Baby Boomer Women: Secure Futures or Not?" the *Harvard Generations Policy Journal* and the Global Generations Policy Institute, 2000.

4. Daily, Nancy, *When Baby Boom Women Retire* (Westport: Praeger, 2000), p. 7.

5. U.S. Department of Labor Women's Bureau Quick Stats 2005, http://www.dol.gov/wb/stats/main.htm.

6. Daily, *When Baby Boom Women Retire*, p. 57.

The assumption that ten million Boomer women are likely to receive rewards beyond money is based on the data that ten million Boomer women are college graduates.

7. Green, Brent, *Marketing to Leading Edge Boomers* (New York: Writers Advantage, 2003), p. 49.

8. Friedan, Betty, *The Feminine Mystique* (New York: W. W. Norton & Co., 2001), p. 20.

9. Ibid., p. 22.

10. Ibid., p. 15.

11. Strauss, William, and Howe, Neil, *Generations: The History of America's Future, 1584–2069* (New York: Quill, 1991), p. 284.

12. http://www.cwluherstory.com/CWLUAArchive/crcwlu.html.

13. E-mail from Project Renewment member Barbara Hammer, Ph.D., to Karen Koch, *Los Angeles Times* journalist, August 24, 2005.

14. Atchley, Robert C., *The Sociology of Retirement* (Cambridge: Schenkman Publishing Company, 2002), p. 53.

15. Based on the experience of Helen Dennis, who has worked with more than ten thousand employees preparing for the nonfinancial aspects of their retirement.

16. Price, Christine, "Women and Retirement: Relinquishing Professional Identity," *Journal of Aging Studies* 14, no. 1 (2002), p. 83.

17. Bauer-Maglin and Radosh, *Women Confronting Retirement*, p. 6.

18. Based on the experience of Helen Dennis, who has worked with more than ten thousand employees preparing for the nonfinancial aspects of their retirement.

19. Price, Christine, "Retirement for Women: The Impact of Employment," *Journal of Women and Aging* 14 (3/4), p. 47.

20. Ibid., pp. 41–57.

21. Ibid., p. 47.

22. Ibid., p.50.

23. Ibid., p. 51.

24. Reprint of the commencement address of John W. Gardner to graduates from the University of Southern California, June 10, 1965.

25. Ibid.

2: I WON'T EARN ANOTHER DOLLAR

1. Pollan, Stephen M., and Levine, Mark, *Die Broke: A Radical, Four-Part Financial Plan* (New York: HarperBusiness, 1997), p. 48.

2. http:///www.cbo.gove/showdoc.cfm?index=5195&sequence=0.

3. Ibid.

4. Mellan, Olivia, *Money Harmony* (New York: Walker and Company, 1994), p. 125.

5. http://www.aarp.org/research/socialsecurity/benefits/dd126_women.html.

6. http://financialplan.about.com/library/weely/aa060299.htm.

7. Resnick, Judy, with Stone, Gene, *I've Been Rich. I've Been Poor. Rich Is Better* (New York: Golden Books, 1993), p. 5.

3: CHANGE IS THE NORM

1. *Wall Street Journal,* June 7, 1967, http://www.bartleby.com/63/49/2249.html. King Whitney Jr. was president of Personnel Laboratories, Inc. This was taken from his presentation at a sales meeting.

5: I ONLY CRY AT THE MOVIES

1. Downey, Charles, "Health Information: Toxic Tears; How Crying Keeps You Healthy" (Brigham and Women's Hospital, a teaching affiliate of Harvard Medical School. Found in http://www.thirdage.com/healthgate/files/14240.html).

2. Ibid.

3. Ibid.

4. Ibid.

5. Ibid.

6. http://www.pbs.org/newshour/bb/remember/muskie.3-26.html.

7. Downey, "Health Information: Toxic Tears."

8. Ibid.

9. http://www.pbs.org/newshour/essays/fleming_7-10.html.

10. Ibid.

11. Ibid.

12. Ibid.

13. Ibid.

14. Ibid.

15. http://en.thinkexist.com/quotation/if_you_haven-t_cried-your_eyes_can-t_be_beautiful/219979.html

16. Parachin, Victor, "Fears About Tears," *Vibrant Life* (November/December 1992), http://www.findarticles.com/p/articles/mi_m0826/is_n6_v8/ai_12939494.

6: WHO AM I WITHOUT A BUSINESS CARD?

1. http://www.greatfxbusinesscards.com/articles/using-business-cards-to-network-market.htm.

2. http://www.belightsoft.com/prodcuts/composer/history19.php.

3. Albright, Madeleine, *Madame Secretary: A Memoir* (New York: Miramax Books, 2003), p. 340.

7: ADDICTED TO POWER

1. http://www.google.com/search?hl=en&lr=&ie+UtF-8&defl=en&q=define:Addictions&sa=.

2. http://www.workaholics-anonymous.org.

8: LESS STEAM IN MY ENGINE

1. This statement was overheard by Helen Dennis when she was a board member of a nonprofit organization.

2. http://www.ingnycmarathon.org/training/dtip03/php.

3. http://www3.thinkexist.com/quotation/insanity-doing_the_same_thing_over_and_over_again/15511.html.

4. http://quotations.about.com/cs/inspirationquotes/a/Energy2.htm.

9: WORK *AND* RETIREMENT

1. AARP, *Staying Ahead of the Curve: 2003: The AARP Working in Retirement Study,* Washington, D.C.: AARP, 2003.

2. The New Merrill Lynch Retirement Study (2006), www.ml.com/media/66482.com.

3. http://www.quoteworld.org/quotes/5016.

4. http://www.princetonreview.com/cte/profiles/dayInLife.asp?careerID=53.

10: FEELING VULNERABLE

1. Andrews, Robert A., *Cassell Dictionary of Contemporary Quotations* (New York: Sterling Publishing Co., Inc., 1996), p. 420. Originally quoted in *Oprah!* by Robert Waldron (New York: St. Martin's Press, 1987), "A Day with Oprah."

11: ANTIAGING OR PRO-AGING

1. Dennis, Helen, "Evolution of the Link Between Business and Aging," *Generations,* Winter 2004–2005, p. 10.

2. Weiss. J. J., "Chasing Youth," *American Demographics*, October 2002, p. 39.

3. Ibid., pp. 39–41.

4. The Anti-Ageism Taskforce at The International Longevity Center. *Ageism in America*, report by Robert Butler, New York, 2006.

5. http://www.worldhealth.net//96/358.html.

6. Olshansky, S. Jay, Hayflick, Leonard, and Carnes, Bruce A., "No Truth to the Fountain of Youth," *Scientific American*, June 2002.

7. Ibid.

8. Dennis, Helen, "Anti-aging Has Supporters and Detractors," *Daily Breeze*, April 25, 2002.

9. Haas, Jane Glenn, *Time of Your Life: Why Almost Everyone Gets Better After Fifty* (Santa Ana: Seven Locks Press, 2000), p. 6.

10. Ibid.

11. Ibid., p. 16.

12: IS BUSY BETTER?

1. Atchley, Robert C., *Social Forces and Aging*, 6th edition (Belmont: Wadsworth Publishing Co., 1991), p. 210.

2. http://www.thefreedictionary.com/Puritan.

3. Ibid.

4. Ibid.

5. http://abcnews.go.com/print?id=2151399.

6. Atchley, *Social Forces and Aging*, p. 209.

7. Ibid.

8. Andrews, Robert A., *Cassell Dictionary of Contemporary Quotations* (New York: Sterling Publishing Co., 1996), p. 139.

9. http://thinkexist.com/quotes/with/keyword/opinion/.

13: MORE THAN THE BLUES

1. http://www.nimh.nih.gov/publicat/depression.cfm.

2. Ibid.

3. Murray, C. J. L., and Lopez, A. D., eds., "The Global Burden of Disease and Injury Series," *Volume 1: A Comprehensive Assessment of Mortality and Disability from Diseases, Injuries, and Risk Factors in 1990 and Projected to 2020*, Harvard School of Public Health and the World Bank (Cambridge: Harvard University Press, 1996).

4. http://www.aarp.org/health/staying_healthy/prevention/a2003-03-13-depression.html/tools/.

5. Ibid.

6. The Brown University Long-Term Care Quality Advisor, vol. 9, n. 13 (July 14, 1997), p. 5 (from National Mental Health Association website article entitled "Depression and Older Adults").

7. Ibid.

8. Atchley, Robert C., "Selected social and psychological differences between men and women in later life," *Journal of Gerontology* 31 (1076), pp. 204–21.

9. Kim, Jungmeen E., and Moen, Phyllis, "Retirement Transitions, Gender, and Psychological Well-Being," *The Journal of Gerontology Series B: Psychological Sciences and Social Sciences* (2002), pp. P212–P222.

10. Ibid.

11. http://www.wrongdiagnosis.com/d/depression/stats-country.htm (China has a higher estimated rate of depression than the United States).

12. http://www.nimh.nih.gov/publicat/elderlydepsuicide.cfm?Output=Print.

13. http://www.niapublication.org/engagepages/depression.asp.

14. Styron, William, *Darkness Visible: A Memoir of Madness* (New York: Vintage Books, 1992), p. 84.

14: BACK TO THE KITCHEN

1. Burrell, Barbara C., *A Women's Place Is in the House: Campaigning for Congress in the Feminist Era* (Ann Arbor: University of Michigan Press, 1994).

2. Andrews, Robert A., *Cassell Dictionary of Contemporary Quotations* (New York: Sterling Publishing, 1996), p. 102.

15: GOING IT ALONE

1. Straus, Jillian, "Lone Stars: Being Single," *Psychology Today,* May/June 2006, http://www.psychologytoday.com/articles/pto-20060424-000003.html (10/25/06).

2. http:www.aoa.gove/prof/Statistics/statistics.asp.

3. Ibid.

4. U.S. Bureau of the Census (2005). "A Profile of Older Americans," http://www.aoa.gov/PROF/Statistics/profile/2005/5.asp.

16: PASSION: IT'S MORE THAN A FRUIT

1. Stein, Jess, ed., *Random House Dictionary Unabridged* (New York: Random House, 1970), p. 1054.

2. Hudson, Frederic M., and McLean, Pamela D., *Life Launch* (California: Hudson Institute Press, 2001), pp. 68–69.

3. Ibid., pp. 70–71.

4. Bridges, William, *Transitions* (Menlo Park: Addison Wesley Publishing Co., 1980), p. 18.

5. Nathaniel Branden is the author of several books on the subject, including *The Psychology of Self-Esteem, How to Raise Your Self-Esteem* (Hoboken: Jossen-Bass, 1987), and *The Six Pillars of Self-Esteem* (New York: Bantam Books, 1994).

6. Branden, Nathaniel, "Passion and Soulfulness," in *Handbook of the Soul.* Carlson and Benjamin Shield, eds. (New York: Little, Brown, 1994), p. 99.

7. Ibid., p. 100.

8. Ibid.

9. Ibid., p. 85.

17: YOU CAN ALWAYS VOLUNTEER

1. Greene, Kelly, "Avoiding the Volunteer Trap," *Encore: The Journal Report, Wall Street Journal*, April 24, 2006, p. R1.
2. Ibid.
3. Ibid., p. R3.
4. Ibid.
5. Price, Christine, A., "Retirement for Women: The Impact of Employment," *Journal of Women & Aging* 14 (3/4), p. 50.
6. Ibid.

18: WHAT DO I WEAR WHEN I AM NOT IN A BUSINESS SUIT?

1. http:www.cottoninc.com/lsmarticles/?articleIS=169.
2. Streater, Amie, "Midriff-Baring Tops on 50-Year-Olds?" Knight Ridder Newspapers, June 7, 2006, http://www.stltoday.com/stltoday/emaf.nsf/Popup?ReadForm&db=stltoday%5Clifestyle%5.
3. D'Innocenzio, Anne, "Going After the 35-Plus Consumer, Retailers Tryout New Clothing Store Concepts," Associated Press, September 27, 2004, http://global.factive.com/en/arch/print_results.asp.
4. Rozhon, T., "Guess Tries to Regain Its Fabulousness," *New York Times*, September 25, 2004.
5. Byrne, Robert, *1,911 Best Things Anybody Ever Said* (New York: Ballantine Books, 1988), p. 180.

19: GRANDCHILDREN: FINDING THE BALANCE

1. Thomas, William H., *What Are Older People For? How Elders Will Save the World* (Massachusetts: VanderWyk & Burnham, 2004), p. 52.
2. Ibid., p. 53.
3. Ibid.
4. http://www.presideny.ucsb.edu/ws/index.php?pid=32826.

20: THE QUEEN OF MULTITASKING IS TAKING A BREAK

1. http://www.time.com/time/magazine/article/0,9171,1174696-2,00.html.
2. Criss, Brandy R., "Gender Differences in Multitaking" (Missouri Western State University), http://clearinghouse.missouriwestern.edu/manuscripts/815.asp, retrieved September 18, 2006.
3. Ibid. Shellenbarger, S., "Juggling Too Many Tasks Could Make You Stupid," *Career Journal*, http://clearinghouse.missouriwestern.edu/manuscripts/815.asp, retrieved September 18, 2006.
4. Ibid. Williams, C. L., and Meck, W. H., "Organizational Effects or Early Gonodal Secretions on Sexual Differentiation in Spatial Memory," *Behavioral Neuroscience*, 104 (1), pp. 84–97, http://clearinghouse.missouriwestern.edu/manuscripts/815.asp, retrieved September 18, 2006.

5. Ibid. Original source from Halpern, D., "Sex differences in Cognitive Abilities," Mahway, N.J.: Lawrence Erlbaum Associates, 2000, http://clearinghouse.missouri western.edu/manuscripts/815.asp, retrieved September 18, 2006.

6. Anderson, P., "2001 Study: Multitasking Is Counterproductive," CNN.com, http://archives.cnn.com/2001/CAREER/trends/08/05/multitasking.study.

21: DEALING WITH ILLNESS

1. http://www.ncbi.nlm.gov/entrez/query.fcgi.

2. Additional websites: http://www.mic.ki.se/Diseases/index.html.

http://www.merck.com/mmpe/index.html.

http://pdrhealth.com.

http://www.fda.gov.

http://www/reutershealth.com/en/index.html.

http://drkoop.com/home/93/default.html.

http://www.drweil.com/drw/ecs/index.html.

http://cancerweb.ncl.ac.uk/omd.

http://search.looksmart.com/p/search?qt=Prescription+Drugs+Listed+A-Z.

3. In general, a clinical depression is serious and typically cannot be willed away. In this case the woman managed her depression in a way that was effective for her.

22: PERSONAL PLANNING: IS IT FOR ME?

1. Sedlar, Jeri, and Miners, Rick, *Don't Retire, Rewire!* (Indiana: Alpha Books, 2003), p. 48.

2. Information is based on retirement education and planning programs conducted by Helen Dennis for more than ten thousand employees from corporations and universities.

23: WHAT IF *HE* RETIRES FIRST?

1. Moen, Phyllis; Kim, Jungmeen E.; and Hofmeister, Heather, "Couples' Work/Retirement Transitions, Gender, and Marital Quality," *Social Psychology Quarterly* 64, no. 1 (March 2001), pp. 55–71.

2. Trafford, Abigail, "When Spouse Retires, Real Work Begins," *Washington Post*, October 25, 2005, http://www.washingtonpost.com/wp-dyn/content/article/2005/10/24/AR2005102402019.html.

3. Moen, Jungmeen and Hofmeister, "Couples' Work/Retirement Transitions, Gender, and Marital Quality," p. 55.

4. Based on work by Helen Dennis providing retirement educations programs to more than ten thousand employees.

5. Ibid.

6. http://www.brainyquote.com/quotes/quotes/b/benjaminfr123487.html.

24: PLAY

1. http://www.google.com/search?hl=en&lr=UTF-8&defl=en&q=define:play&sa=X&oi=glossary_definition&ct=title.

2. http://www.interactives.co.uk/quotation%20kit.htm.

3. http://www.strongmuseum.org.

4. http://www.proactivehealthnet/healthBB/showthread.php?t=4270 http://www.heylady.com/rbc/laughter.htm.

5. Ibid.

6. http://humormatters.com/articles/researchresults.htm.

25: BUYING THE PLOT

1. Kinzbrunner, Barry M.; Weinreb, Neil J.; and Policzer, Joel S., *20 Common Problems: End-of-Life Care* (New York: McGraw-Hill Professional, 2001), p. 301.

2. Kübler-Ross, Elisabeth, *On Death and Dying* (New York: Simon & Schuster, 2001).

3. Healthcare and Elder Law Programs Corporation, Second Edition, "Your Way: A Guide to Help You Stay in Charge of Decisions About Your Medical Care," Torrance, Calif.: H.E.L.P., www.help4srs.org.

27: SEX: LEST WE FORGET

1. http://www.rjgeib.com/thoughts/franklin/Franklin.html.

2. Ibid.

3. Ibid.

4. Butler, Robert N., and Lewis, Myrna I., *The New Love and Sex After 60* (New York: Ballantine Books, 2002), p. 3.

5. Sheehy, Gail, *Sex and the Seasoned Woman* (New York: Random House, 2006), p. 318.

6. Ibid., p. 319.

7. Butler and Lewis, *The New Love and Sex After 60*, p. 34.

8. Ibid., p. 334.

28: I LOST MY KEYS AND MY CAR

1. Small, Gary, *The Memory Bible* (New York: Hyperion, 2002), p. 64.

2. Ibid.

3. http://www.intelihealth.com/IHihtPrint/WSIHW00031937/31397/347125.html?d=dmtC (reviewed by the faculty of Harvard Medical School).

4. Cohen, Gene, *The Mature Mind: The Positive Power of the Aging Brain* (New York: Basic Books, 2004), p. 3.

5. http://www.businessweek.com/magazine/content/06_39/b4002100.htm?chan=tc&campaign_id=rss_tech.rss091506a.

6. Small, Gary, *The Memory Prescription* (New York: Hyperion, 2004), pp. 33–101.

7. Ibid., p. 7.

8. Small, Gary, *The Memory Bible* (New York: Hyperion, 2002), p. 48.

9. Ibid.

10. Ibid.

11. http://www3.thinkexist.com/quotation/when_i_was_younger_i_could_remember_anything/215898.html.

29: PUSHING SIXTY

1. Loviglio, Joann, "No Pain, No Gain May Not Be Good Advice," Associated Press, Philadelphia, October 24, 2005, U.S. Consumer Product Safety Commission.

2. http://www.niapublications.org/exercisebook/chapt1.htm.

3. Ibid.

4. Ibid.

5. http://capitalhealthcare.ca/YourHealth/BrowseByAlpha/content.asp?L=&NavType=Alpha&guid=DFE4AB7E-3F1F-47C8-8FC3-3C39DB036B30&PageTitle=Tips%20For%20Sticking%20With%20An%20Exercise%20Program&.

6. Stein, Jeannine, "Where They Fit In," *Los Angeles Times*, October 30, 2006.

7. Ibid.

8. http://archives.cnn.com/2002/HEALTH/04/07/americans.exercise/index.html.

9. http://www.niapublicationsorg/exercisebook/intro.htm.

10. Treen, Joe, "Live Longer," *AARP The Magazine*, September/October 2006, p. 83.

11. http://www.quotegarden.com/exercise.html.

30: LOSING A MATE

1. During the time of Project Renewment meetings, several women lost their husbands. This essay reflects their experiences. Women in other long-term relationships whose partners have died may have similar reactions.

2. Crenshaw, David Q., *Bereavement: Counseling the Grieving Throughout the Life Cycle* (New York: The Crossroad Publishing Co., 1996), p. 146.

3. These dos and don'ts are based on the contribution of women who were part of a bereavement group sponsored by Trinity Care Hospice at the Beach Cities Health District, in Torrance, California. They also were part of a weekly column, "Successful Aging," by Helen Dennis in the *Daily Breeze*, a newspaper in the South Bay of Southern California, in an article titled "Surviving Spouses Need Support and Friendship, Not Advice," May 13, 2004.

31: HONORING OUR WISDOM

1. http://www.walgreens.com/about/careers/recruiting/default.jsp.

2. Carter, Jimmy, *The Virtues of Aging* (New York: Ballantine Publishing Co., 1998), p. 13.

3. Cohen, Gene D., *The Creative Age* (New York: Avon Books, 2000), p. 77.

4. Ibid.

5. Bortz, Walter N., *Living Longer for Dummies* (New York: Hungry Minds, 2002), p. 184.

6. Cohen, Gene D., *The Mature Mind: The Positive Power of the Aging Brain* (New York: Basic Books, 2005), p. 95.

7. Ibid.

8. http://cn.wikipedia.org/wiki/Wisdom.

9. Cohen, *The Mature Mind: The Positive Power of the Aging Brain*, pp. 105–6.

10. Ibid., p. 106.

11. Dormann, H. O., *The Speaker's Book of Quotations* (New York: Ballantine Publishing Co., 2000), p. 268.

12. Bolen, J. S., *Goddess in Older Women*, (New York: HarperCollins, 2001), p. xiv.

13. http://www.worldofquotes.com/author/Mark-Twain/1/index.html.

32: THE ILLUSION OF FREEDOM

1. Trafford, Abigail, *My Time: Making the Most of the Rest of Your Life* (New York: Basic Books, 2004).

2. Goldman, Connie, *The Gifts of Caregiving: Stories of Hardship, Hope and Healing* (Minneapolis: Fairview Press, 2002), p. 7.

3. Ibid.

4. *Caregiving in the U.S.* by the National Alliance for Caregiving and AARP, January 2003.

5. Ibid.

6. *Caregiving in the U.S.* by the National Alliance for Caregiving and AARP, April 2004, p. 8.

7. Ibid.

8. Capossela, Cappy, and Warnock, Sheila, *Share the Care: How to Organize a Group to Care for Someone Who Is Seriously Ill* (New York: Simon & Schuster, 1995).

9. Feinberg, L. F.; Horvath, J.; Hunt, G.; and Plooster, L.; Kagan, J.; Levine, C.; Lynn, J.; Mintz, S.; Wilkinson, A., "Family Caregiving and Public Policy Principles for Change," December 1, 2003 (written by a collaborative group of caregiver advocates).

10. Ibid.

11. *The MetLife Caregiving Cost Study: Productivity Losses to U.S. Business* (July 2006). MetLife Mature Market Institute, National Alliance for Caregiving, p. 4.

12. http://www.eldercarecalculator.orgECalc.asp.

13. Goldman, C., *The Gifts of Caregiving*, p. 178.

33: CONNECTING TO MY SOUL

1. Mitroff, Ian I., and Denton, Elizabeth A., *A Spiritual Audit of Corporate America: A Hard Look at Spirituality, Religion, and Values in the Workplace* (San Francisco: Jossey-Bass, 1999), p. 5.

2. Ibid., p. 24.

3. Ibid., p. 5.

4. *Encyclopedia of Aging, 3rd Edition*, George Maddox, ed., 2001, "Spirituality" by Robert P. Atchely, p. 975.

5. Hanh, Thich Nhat, *Peace Is in Every Step* (New York: Bantam Books, 1991), p. ix.

6. Murdock, Maureen, *The Heroine's Journey* (Boston: Shambhala, 1990), p. 6.

7. *Encyclopedia of Aging, 3rd Edition*, George Maddox, ed., p. 975.

34: I CAN LEAVE MY HOUSE, BUT NOT MY HAIRDRESSER

1. AARP Knowledge Management (April 2005). Retirement Migration in the 2000 Census, http://www.aarp.org/research/reference/publicopinions/migration.html.

2. Boyer, Richard, and Savageau, David, *Retirement Places Rated* (New York: Prentice Hall Press, 1987), p. 1.

35: JOY

1. http://www.simonsays.com/content/book/cfm?tab=15&pid=40757.

2. http://jcgi.pathfinder.com/time/archive/printout/0,23657,918499,00.html.

3. http://en.wikipedia.org/wiki/Joy,_Illinois.

4. *Webster's Seventh New Collegiate Dictionary* (Springfield, Mass.: G. C. Merriam Company, 1970), p. 459.

Similar to Webster's dictionary definition, scientists have equated joy with happiness, a legitimate field of scientific inquiry. Three thousand papers have been published in the *Journal of Happiness Studies*, accompanied by a World Database of Happiness. In 2005, Great Britain's Royal Institution hosted a debate among three academicians on the topic of "Happiness, the Science Behind Your Smile." At the London School of Economics, a noted economist and psychiatrist debated the politics of happiness. In the United States, Martin Seligman, an eminent professor of psychology who coined the phrase "learned helplessness," refocused his research and career on happiness and authored the bestselling book *Authentic Happiness*.

36: WITH A LITTLE HELP FROM MY FRIENDS

1. Goodman, Ellen, and O'Brien, Patricia, *I Know Just What You Mean: The Power of Friendships in Women's Lives* (New York: Simon & Schuster, 2000).

2. Ibid., p. 37.

3. Ibid., p. 280.

4. Ibid.

5. Ibid., p. 53.

6. Taylor, E. T.; Klein, L. C.; Lewis, B. P.; Gruenewald, T. L.; Gurung, R. A. R.; and

Updegraff, J. A., "Biobehavioral Responses to Stress in Females: Tend and Befriend, Not Fight or Flight," *Psychological Review* 107, no. 3 (2000), pp. 411–29.

7. Berkowitz, G., "UCLA Study on Friendship Among Women," 2002, http://www.anapside.org/cnd/gender/tendfend.html.

8. Ibid.

9. Michael, Yvonne L.; Berkman, Lisa F.; Colditz, G.; Graham, A.; and Kawachi, Ichiro, "Living Arrangement, Social Integration, and Change in Functional Health Status," *American Journal of Epidemiology* 153(2), January 2001, pp. 123–31 (Nurses' Health Study, Harvard Medical School).

37: A SORORITY HOUSE, NOT A NURSING HOME

1. Brown, L. B., "In California, New Kind of Commune for Elderly," *New York Times*, February 28, 2006.

2. Ibid.

3. Gross, Jane, "Aging at Home: For a Lucky Few, a Wish Come True," *New York Times*, February 9, 2006.

4. Ibid.

5. http://aspe.hhs.gov/daltcp/reports/NORCssp.htm.

6. Older Americans Update 2006: Key Indicators of Well-Being, p. 52; Federal Interagency Forum on Aging Related Statistics, Washington, D.C.

7. Thomas, William H., *Life Worth Living: How Someone You Love Can Still Enjoy Life in a Nursing Home—The Eden Alternative in Action* (Massachusetts: VanderWyk & Burnham, 1996). See http://www.edenalt.org and http://www.ncaonline.org/ncpad/eden.shtml.

8. Thomas, *Life Worth Living*. See http://www.ncbcapitalimpact.org/default.aspx ?id=148.

9. http://www.ncbcapitalimpact.org/default.aspx?id=148.

38: AUTHENTICITY

1. Chodron, Pema, *The Wisdom of No Escape* (Boston: Shambala, 2001), p. 8.
2. Ibid.
3. http://en.wikipedia.org/wiki/Authenticity_(philosophy).
4. http://www.quotedb.com/quotes/1573.

ABOUT THE AUTHORS

⊡ ⊡ ⊡

BERNICE BRATTER

A native Angeleno, Bernice graduated from UCLA with a major in psychology. She did graduate work at the Phillips Graduate Institute, where she obtained a master's degree in social science. She is a licensed marriage and family therapist and has served as president of the Los Angeles Women's Foundation, a public foundation dedicated to reshaping the lives of girls and women in Southern California, as well as executive director of the Center for Healthy Aging, a nonprofit interdisciplinary health care organization for older adults and their families.

An advocate on aging and women's issues, she has appeared in front of various government agencies and has lectured and served as a consultant to nonprofit organizations. In 1981 she was a gubernatorial appointee as observer for the State of California to the White House Conference on Aging and is the recipient of numerous awards and commendations including the Santa Monica YWCA Woman of the Year Award as well as the Center for Healthy Aging Community Leader Award.

Bernice holds an honorary doctor of law degree from Pepperdine University and has served on the board of directors of Tenet Healthcare. She has appeared on *60 Minutes, 20/20, The Phil Donahue Show* and in *Hour Detroit* magazine. In 1999 she cofounded Project Renewment, which explores the different challenges career women face once they leave the workforce.

As cofounder of Project Renewment she continues to meet the demand of women who want to join a Project Renewment group. Since her retirement in 2000 she has kept up her interests in writing, reading, grandparenting, traveling, physical fitness, cultural activities and ongoing education. She enjoys her children and grandchildren and resides in Los Angeles with her husband.

HELEN DENNIS

Helen Dennis is a nationally recognized leader on issues of aging, employment and retirement. She has conducted research on these issues for organizations such as The Conference Board, AARP, UC Berkeley and the U.S. Administration on Aging. Nationally, she has lectured extensively to the business community, professional groups, nonprofit organizations and government agencies.

In her consulting practice Helen has worked with more than ten thousand employees planning the nonfinancial aspects of their retirement, including men and women who are senior executives, managers, factory workers and university faculty and staff. She is the editor of two books, *Retirement Preparation* and *Fourteen Steps in Managing an Aging Work Force*, and a weekly columnist writing on "Successful Aging" for *The Daily Breeze*, a MediaNews group newspaper.

As a leader, Helen has served as president of three nonprofit organizations and currently serves as chairperson for the American Society on Aging's Business Forum on Aging and the Healthcare and Elder Law Programs in Southern California. She was appointed as a delegate to the 2005 White House Conference on Aging and serves on the national board of the American Society on Aging.

A lecturer for more than twenty years at the University of Southern California's Andrus Gerontology Center, she has been the recipient of several awards for her teaching effectiveness and contributions to the field of aging. These include the Distinguished Teaching Award from the Association for Gerontology in Higher Education, the Excellence in Teaching Award from the Andrus Associates at the University of Southern California and the Francis Townsend Award in Gerontology from California State University, Long Beach.

Her views on age, employment and retirement issues have been quoted by the *Wall Street Journal*, the *Los Angeles Times*, the *Christian Science Monitor*, the *Sacramento Bee* and others. She has also appeared on *20/20* and national network news programs.

As cofounder of Project Renewment, she continues to support the formation of Project Renewment groups and has made numerous national presentations on the challenges and opportunities facing career women in retirement.

She enjoys reading, travel and theater as well as yoga, Pilates and running. A resident of Redondo Beach, California, Helen treasures the time she spends with her children and grandchildren, who also live in Southern California.